AMPHIBIAN

AMPHIBIAN

The Adventures of a Professional Diver

by JIM GOTT
with Norman Lewis Smith

ΨP

A PLAYBOY PRESS BOOK

Library of Congress Cataloging in Publication Data

Gott, Jim.
    Amphibian: the adventures of a professional diver.

    1. Scuba diving. I. Smith, Norman Lewis, joint author. II. Title.
VM989.G67   797.2'3 [B]   75-45072
ISBN 0-87223-462-2

To Pat Graber

CONTENTS

PREFACE

In the 17 years since I discovered the underwater world, I have been scuba diving in many places, under many circumstances: in New York City's East River as a boy, in Vietnam with the Marines, in the Gulf of Mexico as a commercial diver, in the Caribbean and around Bermuda as a dive tour director, and from the West Coast to the Mediterranean for my own pleasure.

Each dive has been an adventure. It's such a new and different world down there that there's always something exciting to learn, to see, to experience. When I'm beneath the surface of the ocean, I have a sense of freedom and tranquility that I've found nowhere else. No drugs are needed for consciousness heightening underwater because the environment itself is mind expanding—and it's real. Free of gravity, I slowly descend through the water; controlling my buoyancy, I hover for a moment, then float soft as a feather into a ship that has lain on the bottom of the sea for centuries. That's my high. And that's what I want to share with others.

When I began diving, the underwater world was a relatively private one. The sport of scuba was still in its infancy. Now the fraternity of divers has grown into the millions, and as a scuba instructor, I help increase that number every year.

When I dive, I feel at one with the ocean; it is my element almost as much as land is. A fish swims up and peers into my face mask and I nod a hello, because I belong down there with the porpoises and periwinkles, the anemones and the abalones. Even if a zoologist wouldn't consider me one, I feel that I am an amphibian; I belong to two separate worlds, one dry and one wet.

Too many divers retain a sense of being aliens when they venture underwater, even after years of diving. Like the language teacher who wants his students to stop translating every word in their heads and begin thinking in the foreign language, I try to get my students to stop thinking as land beings and start thinking as divers. I want them to feel as at home in the underwater world as I do.

I've used different scuba textbooks in my classes and have recommended various scuba guidebooks. But these mostly tell the reader how to dive or where to dive, not what it's really like down there. I've always believed the adage that experience is the best teacher, and that the next best is vicarious experience. When I was in school, I always learned most when I could live the event being taught in my imagination —whether it was crossing the Delaware with Washington, or working with Louis Pasteur in his laboratory.

In teaching scuba, I've found that the best way for me to convey a point about diving is to relate it to my own experiences. I'm extroverted enough to enjoy telling stories about myself. But, more important, I want my students not only to know the facts and techniques of scuba diving but also to have a sense of the world they're entering and what to expect of it.

That's what I've tried to do in this book. I'm not writing as an expert because I feel that there are no experts on this frontier; it's still too new and unexplored. I write simply as someone who has had many different experiences under the seas that may interest and inform the reader and encourage him to explore this fascinating world for himself. I take the reader through my own education as a diver, so he or she can share my adventures and learn from my mistakes.

I hope that this book is both entertaining and useful to all those interested in the underwater world.

For background information on many of the subjects covered, I've used a number of sources, including *Skin Diver Magazine;* John E. Kenny, *Business of Diving* (New York: Gulf Publishing Company, 1972); Judy Gail May, *Scuba Diver's Guide to Underwater Ventures* (Harrisburg: Stackpole Books, 1973); and Richard A. Frank, "Law At Sea," *New York Times Magazine,* May 18, 1975.

I've used actual names in this book except for cases where the people might be embarrassed or I've simply forgotten the name.

My thanks to all who contributed photos to this book, with a special thank you to Joe Payne, Don Arrington and Bill Gleason who spent many hours sorting, developing and printing the photos. I am also indebted to John Hilbert for his continued support throughout the years.

AMPHIBIAN

CHAPTER 1

GETTING WET

Last spring a woman came into the Skin Diving School of New York to enroll her 13-year-old son in my scuba class. I groaned to myself, a kid that young is going to complicate things. My teaching methods, my stories, my jokes are geared to adult students, not children.

I explained that it was against the school's policy to teach scuba diving to someone under 16, unless one of his parents was taking the class, because we believe children need adult supervision. The woman, who I later learned was a widow and a doctor, said that she had no time to learn diving herself. Her son had already begun diving in a summer camp and with family friends, and now he wanted to take a course to get his diver's certification card. The woman seemed so anxious for her son to learn diving from our course that I finally enrolled him, after she agreed to sit in on the classes.

Her son, Art, was small, cheerful and very bright. During the first poolside lecture, when I talked about Archimedes' Principle and buoyant forces, I got blank stares from the seven adults in the class. But Art's eyes were flashing, and his hand was waving in the air every minute to ask me another question. He wasn't asking to please me, but because he wanted to learn. Art was the best swimmer in the class and, even more important, I could see that he was totally at home in the water. He wanted to learn diving, and he was excited by it.

After the class I told his mother that she didn't have to attend any more sessions if she didn't want to. I was now glad to have Art in the class, and I knew he would become a good scuba diver.

I knew because Art reminded me of myself. Like Art, I'd become totally absorbed by diving at a very early age.

My diving career began at the age of 11, and I began alone. My early dives were in New York's East River, and my only instruction was from a book. It was 1959, and scuba diving as we know it today was in its first decade. The first aqualungs—self-contained underwater breathing apparatus (SCUBA) developed by Jacques Cousteau—had come to America only in 1950. Today more than two million men and women have been certified as scuba divers by one of the national instruction organizations, and probably well over a million are active in the sport in this country. In 1959 there were probably only 100,000, and I must have been among the youngest and least likely of them all. No one else I knew in the South Bronx had ever used scuba gear. The Bronx is known for producing basketball players, not divers.

I lived at 138th Street, near Bruckner Boulevard, with my parents, an older brother, two older sisters and a grandmother. It was a working class neighborhood with mostly Germans, Italians, Irish and Jews living in the closely packed apartment houses, though blacks and Puerto Ricans were starting to become part of the mix. My father worked for the New York Central Railroad, and we lived on the fourth floor of a five-story walkup. Our family was close, but it was crowded in the apartment, so I spent my time on the streets of the neighborhood. I played stickball and football and learned street smarts, which generally meant using your wits to avoid getting your head bashed in.

I got into diving through a combination of things: First, my sense of adventure as a boy was always leading me into some new activity where I could test myself and maybe even learn something. Sometimes I got into new activities with my friends, but I didn't mind doing things alone. Another reason was "Sea Hunt," one of my favorite TV programs. And finally, I loved the water.

I learned to swim at our local Bare Ass Beach, an East River wharf in the industrial section of the South Bronx. It was at the east end of 134th Street. There were few houses in that area; it was mostly factories, coal yards and the oil depots where the tankers came in. We crossed Bruckner Boulevard, walked four or five blocks, and crossed the train yards. We then had to sneak by the security guards at the Paragon Oil Company. If they saw us crossing the yard, they'd chase us, but once we got behind the wharf buildings in back, we were home free. We could see the workers inside through an open hanger door, but they never bothered us.

I started going down to the wharf with my friends when I was eight. But at first I didn't jump in the water with them. I knew my parents wouldn't want me to, and I looked at the oil and garbage floating on the foul-smelling water, and it didn't look very nice. But then one very hot day, my friends were yelling, "Come on, Jimmy, jump in, don't be chicken." I stripped off my clothes and jumped. Filthy or not, I liked the water, though I made sure not to swallow any of it.

It wasn't all deep water. Away from the section where the tankers docked, the bottom sloped out for 15 or 20 feet before dropping off into the channel. But none of us wanted to stay in the shallow water and have all that muck sucking at our feet. I learned to swim very quickly. On a hot summer day you could find me close to the wharf, among the pilings, splashing around with the others, having a grand time. We didn't go out too far because the currents were treacherous in that area. Riker's Island, which housed a prison, was right across from where we swam, and once in a while we'd hear stories about how a prisoner tried to swim to freedom, only to be carried away by the currents and drowned.

Occasionally there'd be a tugboat at the dock with no one on it. We'd run around on the tug, playing tag, until the cops came. Then we'd dive off the side. The cops rarely bothered us otherwise. When no tug was there, one of my favorite spots along the "beach" was the coal chute tower next to the Burns Brothers coal yard. It had ropes hanging from it, and we'd swing out over the water, then plunge in.

The only bad part of the day would be going home. I'd climb out of the water with creosote from the pilings all over me. When I got home, I'd sneak into the bathroom and scrub and scrub to get that stuff off me. I didn't want my parents to know that I was out swimming in the river. My father probably would have shrugged it off, but it would have upset my mother. She was already convinced her youngest son was a little crazy.

A summer or so after I learned how to swim in the East River, my parents bought a one-room cabin and some property on Putnam Lake, just north of the city. On summer weekends we'd go up to picnic, row on the lake, do some swimming and stay overnight on cots in the cabin. One day —I must have been about ten—I saw a diver at the edge of the lake, wearing full scuba gear. I ran down to look him over. I could see that his regulator looked different from the one Mike Nelson (Lloyd Bridges) wore in "Sea Hunt." I realize now that his regulator was one of the early single-hose models that were just beginning to replace the double-hose regulators. I went up to the diver as he was putting his fins on and asked him what he was doing. He said that he was hired by the community to inspect the lake bottom. I followed him into the water and swam on top, watching his bubbles come up, as he swam below. When he came out, I tagged along behind him, not knowing what to say or what to ask him, but not wanting him to get out of my sight.

We only went to the lake on weekends; on summer weekdays and on weekends when we weren't at the lake, my parents began sending me to a boys club in midtown Manhattan, in the East Fifties. The club had a pool and gave swimming lessons, but I never took any, since I already knew how to swim. Never having had proper lessons is probably why I never did become a graceful, stylish swimmer. Early on, though, I had a powerful stroke and endurance; at the lake I could plod along for a mile.

On the way to the club near the Lexington Avenue subway station, I used to pass by a dive shop. It no longer exists, but it must have been one of the original ones in the New York area. I remember the first time I saw it: I was with a group of kids from the neighborhood, and we all stared in the window, fascinated with the equipment on display and the manikin dressed in wet suit, fins, mask, tank and regulator.

My friends eventually lost their interest in the shop, but every day that I went to the club I stopped in front of the shop. Once I wandered in, but when the salesman came up to me and asked what I wanted, I didn't know what to say. Not wanting to admit that I was just looking around, I muttered something and quickly walked out.

At the club, a few of the kids began to bring masks and fins to the pool. I asked how much they cost and borrowed a set to try them out; now I knew something I could get at the dive shop. I saved up enough to buy a cheap mask and set of fins and plunked my money on the dive shop's counter. While others at the pool spent their time having water battles, the group of us with masks would invent retrieving games to test our underwater seeing ability.

What I really wanted, though, was a tank and regulator. Now that I had established myself as a customer at the shop —having bought a scuba book as well as mask and fins—I'd drop in to price tanks and regulators. The cheapest set they had included a 26-cubic-foot-capacity tank—what we'd now call a pony tank or bailout bottle—and cost $29.95. I couldn't ask my parents for the money. I would have gotten clobbered if they knew I was planning to swim underwater wearing an air tank. Besides they couldn't afford to buy me expensive toys, and I felt it was my duty to earn my own spending money.

I earned the money with my shoeshine kit. My friend Kevin and I would work the Erie Bar in my neighborhood. We'd pick out the drunks—not those who were totally out of it, but the ones on the edge—and ask, "Shine 'em up, sir?" The men who got drunk in that bar were usually pretty careless with their money, and they might lay a dollar on me for a 15-cent shine. Maybe they forgot to ask for the change, or they were feeling generous; either way was okay by me. Kevin, who was working toward an English racer, once got a five-dollar bill by accident. He kept his mouth shut and was that much closer to his bike.

Eventually I saved enough. I went down to the shop, not even stopping at the club first. I took the money out of my wallet, so the clerk would know that I was a serious customer, and asked for the $29.95 tank and regulator set. He looked me over, and said, "I can't sell that to you. You're too young."

I ran out of the shop and headed straight for the club. I wasn't about to be stopped now that I had the money. At the club I found Pete, a 16-year-old who lived in my neighborhood and often rode back and forth with me. I explained the situation and he agreed to buy the equipment for me. We walked back to the shop. I handed him the money just before he went in, then I kept my eye on him through the window. Long before I had learned not to trust anyone with my money, but this was an emergency.

Pete came out with the gear, and we made a plan. He'd keep it at his house, which was a block from mine, and he could use it whenever I wasn't using it. When I wanted the tank and regulator, he'd always have it available. That way, my parents would never find out. I wasn't totally at ease with the arrangement, since I was a little leary of Pete. He and his widower father had both had scrapes with the law from time to time. But I had to trust him now.

That night I read and reread my scuba diving book, and about seven the next morning, a Sunday, I slipped out of the apartment and went to Pete's. He lived on the ground floor, so I tapped on his window to wake him up, and he passed the tank and regulator out the window to me.

I lugged the scuba gear two blocks to the Triboro Bridge and took the stairs and pedestrian walkway to Randall's Island. Filled mostly with parks, picnic areas and softball fields, the island is located between the Bronx, Queens and Manhattan, where the Harlem River meets the East River. We used to play softball there. An estuary ran behind the softball fields, and after games we'd sometimes go crabbing there, using broomsticks with nails stuck into them. A couple of times, I had gone swimming in the estuary. It was isolated there, and the water was shallow. I figured it'd be a good place to start my diving.

The morning was warm and sunny, but it was early, so the area was deserted except for a dog walker in the distance. I sat down at the edge of the muddy bank. Glancing through my diving instruction book, I attached the regulator to the tank. I wasn't scared, but my hands trembled with excitement. Finally, I strapped the tank to my back and waded in. When the water was up to my waist, I stuck my head under it—and breathed! It worked! I couldn't see anything except the beer cans and trash floating on the surface, and that made things a little scary. Like every new diver, I had two problems to face: fear of the unknown and lack of confidence in my equipment.

Gradually I relaxed and began swimming under the surface, though no more than a couple of feet down, in case something went wrong. I still couldn't see anything in the polluted water, but I began to feel better and better about it. I was moving underwater, like a frogman, like Mike Nelson, swimming where fish—or at least eels— lived! I was roaming the underwater world, small and dirty as this part of it was.

Then, suddenly, I couldn't breathe. I surfaced immediately and stood there, cursing my luck. My regulator was brand new, could it already be broken? I'd spent my life savings on this thing; it couldn't break yet. I climbed back on the bank and read the instruction book again. I took the regulator off, opened the little valve on the tank, and nothing came out. I'd run out of air, that was the trouble. Now my first dive was at an end, and my next worry was finding a way to get the tank refilled.

When Pete went with me to the boys club, I'd have him go in the dive shop to fill it. But Pete was losing interest in the club and no longer went down there very often. Also, he never seemed to take much interest in the scuba gear. I don't think he used it himself more than once or twice.

A young couple, Sonny and Beverly, lived downstairs from my family's apartment. They were in their twenties; he was a fireman and she stayed at home, though they had no children. I'd run errands for her and hang around their apartment on rainy days. They both took a liking to me, but Sonny worked irregular hours and I would see her more often than him. I think she must have gotten a kick out of the way I was always trying new things. She wasn't my mother, so she didn't have to worry about me. I'd tell her all my adventures, knowing she'd never tell my folks. Of course, I told her about my scuba equipment and the East River dives. The next time I saw Sonny, he asked me about my diving. I told him and mentioned my problem getting air for the tank. He said, "I can take care of that for you." His firehouse had an air compressor for the Scott Airpacs that firemen use. I brought my tank to him and he got it filled at the firehouse.

I continued to keep my life as a frogman secret. I did show off the equipment once in a while to a friend, but I didn't show it to more than a select few or lend it to anyone except Pete. Someone might take too much of a liking to it; and if someone had stolen it, I would have been heartbroken.

Though I didn't realize it at the time, diving was becoming the most important thing in my life.

CHAPTER 2

MARINE TRAINING

"I can't do it, Jimmy!"

"Yes you can. I *know* you can do it, Bill (or Jane or Sam or Mary). Come on, now, try it again."

It always happens in a basic scuba class. A student finds a pool exercise difficult and immediately decides that he or she can't do it. Probably the student has an office job, and it has been years since he has physically pushed himself beyond a few easy games of tennis. He has forgotten, or maybe never knew, that the mind can tell the body what to do even when the body doesn't want to do it.

I don't teach in the old "gorilla" style of scuba instructing. That is, I don't expect every student to turn out to be a UDT diver who can swim five miles nonstop and hold his breath for five minutes. In order to enroll in the class, though, every student must have a doctor's statement saying that he or she is physically capable of taking the course, and every student must prove himself to be at least competent as a swimmer. When a student decides that something is too difficult for him, therefore, I consider it part of my job to teach him how to extend himself, to push beyond what seem to him to be his physical limits. I won't allow him to cop out on himself too easily. I tell him that *I* am confident he can do it. Since I know he can do it, I demand it of him. In response to my confidence and my demands, he goes ahead and does it. Then he is elated. My confidence in him becomes his confidence in himself.

Nothing in a basic scuba course really demands very much strength, coordination or endurance, but it may seem demanding to someone not used to physical exertion. By overcoming his body's reluctance to exert itself, a diver can gain some confidence in his ability to make his body obey his mind. And in more difficult circumstances, he may have the psychological strength not to quit on himself.

Diving is, after all, a physical activity, and a diver can sometimes run—or swim—into difficult situations. I don't ever want a diver with my signature on his certification card to wash up on a beach because he didn't know he could have summoned the strength to keep going when he had to.

You can't learn all of this in a basic or even advanced scuba class, but you can get a sense of it if the teacher makes you push yourself when things seem difficult. I was taught how to push my body to its limits, and then beyond, to the point where it cried out, "This is it, no further." And then I'd push it further, to where I could do things that I'd have sworn were physically impossible for me. My teachers were the experts in this field—Marine Corps drill instructors.

In the spring of 1966, my senior year at Cardinal Hayes High School, I was called into the office of the guidance counselor, a Christian Brother, like most of the faculty. He suggested we have a talk about my future. "Can I smoke?" I asked. Smoking was strictly prohibited in that school, but with a subject as big as my future to discuss, I figured he'd make an exception to the rules. He did.

"Have you gotten your returns from the colleges yet?" he asked. I told him I had, and which colleges had accepted me.

"Which one are you going to?"

"None of them. I'm going into the Marines."

"You're going where?"

"Into the Marines," I repeated.

"The Marines! This is a college preparatory school. Your parents spent good money sending you here, and you're joining the Marines? That's crazy!"

You'd have thought *he* was being sent to Parris Island instead of me. I tried explaining to him the reasons for my decision: I didn't want to go to college until I had some idea of what I wanted to do with a college education; I figured that the Marines would give me some time to think about my future and make some intelligent decision.

"But why the Marines?" he asked. I said I didn't really know, that it just appealed to me; I'd never been a Marine before, so I thought I'd try it.

What I didn't tell him, and admitted only to myself, was that I wanted to prove something to myself. The Marines were supposed to be the toughest branch of service, and I wanted to find out how I'd do as a Marine.

A war was going on. Like most people at the time, especially in my neighborhood, I believed in the war—stop them over there before they get here, and all the rest. But I didn't join the Marines to fight for political reasons. The personal challenge drew me; daring to pit myself against an opponent in a high stakes game of survival where losing meant being killed. I didn't think about it in those terms at the time, but after I came back from Vietnam, I knew that was what, in essence, I was doing. It sounds like, and is, an insanely foolish reason to fight a war, I agree. But it's the type of insanity that many teen-agers and very young men are subject to. That's why they draft the young to fight wars.

Right after graduation day, I walked by a recruiting stand and decided, what the hell, I'll do it now. I went in and signed up under the 120-day delay program, which meant I could pick any day within the next four months to enter. I picked September 14th; that would give me the summer, and by then all my friends who were going to college would be gone.

About a week later I told my parents that I had to talk to them. "Yeah? What about?" my father asked.

"Well, I'll be leaving in September."

"Where are you going?"

"Parris Island. I'm joining the Marines."

"Now listen, I think you'd be a lot better off if you went into the Navy. You could learn a skill and . . ."

"It's too late. I've already joined. I have to leave September fourteenth."

My father thought I was making a mistake, but that didn't surprise him. My mother's reaction was, well, a mother's reaction.

That summer I worked at Lou Feldman's Gaiety Delicatessen in Manhattan. At night our crowd partied, and on weekends we would usually go out to Rockaway Beach. Four of us would rent a bungalow, and 16 of us would sleep there. While the others would be sunbathing on the beach, I would be out beyond the breakers, snorkling and free diving in my mask and fins. But not scuba diving. I hadn't been scuba diving since my early teens.

One weekend I had come home from a family picnic and gone over to Pete's house to pick up my tank and regulator, and Pete wasn't there. The house was empty. Pete and his father had suddenly moved, and Pete had taken my scuba gear with him. I felt crushed. By then, my tank and my regulator had been my most prized possessions.

But I was in my teens, and other things were also becoming important to me. Now that the tank and regulator were gone, and it would take me some time to save up for a new set, their importance faded. An activity that I had to do alone didn't seem as attractive as one I could do with others, especially girls. I did save my money for a new tank and regulator, but by the time I'd earned enough, the summer had ended and I spent my money on my dates. I didn't forget my scuba diving completely, though. I bought books on scuba, and when I went free diving in the summer, I kept telling myself that soon I'd get myself some good scuba gear. But I never did.

In Marine boot camp, the drill instructors try to break you down to nothing and then build you up again the way the Corps wants you to be. And they succeed. In our platoon of 105, we had clodhoppers and city slickers, big shots and nobodies, smart kids and dummies. They started us all off at the same level. Zero. And in case anyone missed the point, there was always a drill instructor at hand to emphasize one's rating in the world, as "maggot" or "shithead."

One day shortly after we arrived the smallest drill instructor, who was about five-foot-eight and wore glasses but was solidly muscled, approached the toughest looking recruit, a reservist attending Michigan State on a football scholarship. "Are you eye-fucking me?" asked the DI, suggesting that the football player was staring at him, which of course he wasn't.

"No, I'm not," replied the football player.

"You're supposed to say, 'No, sir!' " yelled the DI.

Then he proceded to smash the football player from one end of the squad bay, our barracks, to the other. The football player fought back, but was thoroughly beaten. This all took place in front of the rest of the recruits. And the lesson wasn't missed by any of us: If he, superjock, was a zero, then we must be minus numbers.

For the first few days, I remained in a state of shock. From the time we got up at 5:00 A.M. to the time we hit the rack at maybe 1:00 A.M., we were running, running, running. Before I came to Parris Island, I couldn't run one mile in a track suit. Now I was running three miles carrying a field pack filled with 40 pounds of sand, plus my rifle and other equipment, I wasn't physically capable of doing what was being demanded of me, but I didn't have time to feel sorry for myself or wonder what the hell I was doing there. I was too busy doing what they wanted me to do.

What kept us running, pushing beyond our limits, was a very simple element: fear. The Marines teach you that fear can overcome any obstacle. My God, I thought, I'm locked on this island with madmen. Those DIs are totally insane. I'd better do what they tell me, or they might well kill me. I also knew that there was no way off the island except as a Section 8 (mental case), as a Marine or in a plastic bag. If you had a rebellious attitude, then you were put in a motivational platoon, which was twice as bad as a regular platoon. They broke you down one way or another.

After the third or fourth week of the ten-week camp, a physical change came over me. I was in condition, and the running started to seem easy. On a 13-mile run, I'd still puff away for the first two miles, but then I'd get my second wind and it would feel like I could go on for days, my legs just pumping up and down with no effort required. My body was no longer telling me that my—or the DI's—demands on it were impossible to meet. That gave me a confidence in myself physically that I never had before—and that I have never forgotten.

As a teen-ager, I was an easy-going, happy-go-lucky type of boy. I always relied much more on my wits than my strength. I was confident that I could outsmart or out-talk anyone trying to give me trouble. Unless I was cornered, I would avoid a fight. Now I wouldn't waste my time trying to con someone out of fighting with me. I'd just lash out at him and beat him to the punch. That's what Marine training does for you: It gives you such total confidence in yourself physically that you don't think twice about fighting anyone.

My wits got exercised enough in trying to keep the drill instructor's wrath from falling on me. I must have set some kind of record for avoiding punishment. Only once did I get singled out for individual punishment; usually they got your number one to three times a week. On a day when the temperature was well over 100 degrees, I got caught on my way back from a water cooler at the back of a classroom. Drinking from the cooler was strictly forbidden, but the instructor always stepped out of the room for just about exactly three minutes before class—I'd timed it, making a science of studying the DIs' patterns—but this time he came back in 30 seconds early. That got me 500 deep knee bends.

There was another attitude that I—and the other recruits —came out of boot camp with: After this, everything else would be downhill. Nothing could be tougher than the ordeal we were undergoing. Even today I'd rather go through my Vietnam combat experiences again than go through another boot camp. At least in Nam I could release my tensions, fears and frustrations by fighting back.

After the ten weeks of boot camp, we had a two-week leave, which I spent at home. Then I was off to Camp Lejeune in North Carolina. I was no longer a boot Marine; now I was a student Marine. But things didn't get much easier. For three months, in advanced infantry training, I managed even less sleep than I had at Parris Island. We'd be out in the field, on a night ambush, then make an 18-mile forced march back to camp the next day, arriving at one in the morning. We couldn't go to bed until we cleaned our rifles and equipment. That would take until 2:30, and we'd be up again at 6:00. No weekends off, no hanging around a club, no candy, no beer, no relaxation except for twice when they took the whole company to see a movie. It was a very Spartan existence, but that's what the Marine Corps is all about.

Next stop was California for training in jungle tactics. I had my Westpac orders by then, so I knew I was going to Vietnam. When I checked in at the camp, a sergeant told me which bunk I should take. "Yes, sir," I replied. "I'm not a *sir,* I'm a sergeant," he told me. "You're not in boot camp now." That was the first moment I realized I'd finally become a Marine, after all the hell I'd gone through.

One day Walt Huber, a short, reserved Philadelphian I'd gotten to know at Camp Lejeune, came through the barracks trying to raise some money by selling an underwater camera. "Where'd you get this, Walt?" I asked. He told me he was a diver. Immediately I began to rap with him about scuba. Walt was actually the first diver I'd ever met.

Soon after that Walt arranged to spend a weekend with his sister, who lived in Ocean Beach outside of San Diego. Her husband, a Navy officer, was on leave from Vietnam. Walt invited me to join him for the weekend. Walt's brother-in-law, perhaps thinking about what lay ahead of us, was anxious to show us a good time. We arrived Friday night, and on Saturday he took Walt and me over to the Navy base and signed out one of the Navy's sailboats.

The idea of spending a day on the water appealed to me enormously. I asked Walt if he had ever scuba-dived these waters, and while he was telling me he had, his brother-in-law broke in: "The base has scuba equipment. I can sign that out, too." A little later we were sailing out of San Diego Harbor with a sailboat loaded down with tanks.

We pulled into a cove and anchored. Since Walt knew I'd never been on the West Coast before, he told me about the kelp forests, which we don't have in the East. Kelp attaches itself to rocks on the bottom and often grows in thick, jungle-like tangles, to the surface. Walt explained the dangers of getting caught in the forests below and how to work my way free if it happened. Walt also warned me about the sea urchins that live among the kelp and to be wary of the spiney creatures whenever I put my hands or feet down.

I have often thought about that brief lecture. Divers sometimes get themselves into trouble simply by being unfamiliar with an area and its particular hazards. Whenever I find out that one of my students might be doing some diving on the West Coast, I sit down with him and tell him about the problems of diving in kelp forests. Any diver exploring an environment new to him should at least talk with someone about local conditions, or dive with a buddy familiar with the area. In some places, local orientation programs are offered to divers by scuba organizations.

Being underwater again felt very natural to me. The tensions and frustrations of the last few months just washed away in the cool water. I was free, freer than I'd ever been, at peace with myself in a tranquil world. I followed my two buddies through the kelp forests, amazed at the clarity of the water and the size and varied shaped of the kelp.

We spent that afternoon diving, and the next day too. One week later, we were off to Nam. We had to travel light, but I brought one item with me that I still have. It's a small, triangular sandstone rock from that cove, with holes worn into it by the wave action. No craftsman could have fashioned anything so lovely as that rock. I kept it because it reminded me of something very fine and peaceful that I experienced just before beginning a year of war.

CHAPTER 3

VIETNAM, ABOVE AND BELOW WATER

Damaged though it was, I found Vietnam a beautiful country. And after I left I often thought about going back, once the war was over, for a scuba-diving vacation. I did some scuba over there, which I didn't find too enjoyable, given the circumstances, but I thought it might be fun when the guns stopped firing. Now I suppose I'll have to wait until Hanoi invites a U.S. table-tennis team for a visit and relations become friendlier.

I arrived in Vietnam in March 1967 and was assigned to a security platoon, Subunit 2, Headquarters Battalion at Chu Lai, on the South China Sea. Chu Lai was a secure area at the time: "In the rear with the gear," as we called it. We would have guard duty at night and then do odd jobs during the day. They kept us busy, but whenever I had free time I'd spend it at the 100-yard-long strip of beach we had.

Being a Marine in these circumstances was easy enough work, even though a little boring. But the Marine who really had it made was the sergeant in the headquarters unit in charge of recreational equipment. All day long, he'd sit in his thatched hut on the beach, handing out surf boards, volley balls, inflatable rafts.

He didn't have any scuba gear to give out, but I soon found out that he had his own personal gear. I didn't ask to borrow it right away. I knew how reluctant I had been to lend my tank and regulator. First, I became friendly with the sergeant. Then I got him into conversations about diving. Eventually, I asked to borrow his equipment, but he turned me down. Every day I kept bugging him: "Let me borrow it, Sarge, just for one dive. What could happen? I'm a good diver." Finally he gave in.

I put on the gear and headed out. It was a nice feeling, being under the water again. The water was clean, but wave action had kicked up the sand, limiting visibility, so I headed out for clear water. I didn't have a compass, and when I got 100 to 150 yards out, I came up to get my bearings. When I surfaced, I saw a patrol boat with a shark's mouth newly painted on the bow cruising nearby, and I waved. That was the wrong move. The U.S. Navy had just turned over some 25-foot patrol boats to the South Vietnamese and they were out on a shakedown cruise. They were eager to try out their equipment. As soon as they spotted me waving at them, one of the South Vietnamese sailors headed for the machine gun mounted on the bow.

"Hey, I'm one of you guys," I yelled, but when I saw him swing the gun around in my direction, I decided not to argue and made the fastest dive of my career. I reached the bottom, about 30 feet down, before I saw the bullets zapping into the water. Fortunately for me, even 50-caliber machine gun bullets can't penetrate very deep into the water; I could see the tracers of bubbles left by the bullets as they entered the water and then slowed down after eight or nine feet. But that didn't make me feel secure. I was worried that they might have grenades or depth charges, which would have blasted me out of there with no trouble. And even if they didn't, I still couldn't stay down all day. I didn't figure they'd be running out of ammunition anytime soon, and I had to get back to the beach before my air ran out, so I started swimming. I could see the boat following me and the bullets entering the water where my bubbles showed on the surface.

Back on the beach, meanwhile, the sergeant had seen what was happening and was waving frantically at the boat, yelling, "No, no, you're making a mistake." The South Vietnamese were cheerfully waving back, as if to assure him, "It's okay, we got him cornered."

I didn't want to come up on the beach, where I would have been an easy target, so I headed north of the beach, where I could surface among the rocks that jutted out into the water. The only trouble there were the Marines up on the cliff, guarding the general's helipad. I worried that they might make the same mistake the South Vietnamese were making, especially if they saw me being pursued by a "friendly" patrol boat. Since this was a secure area, however, the guards had to request permission from an officer before they could fire at anything. I had thought it a silly rule when I was on guard duty, but now I was grateful for it.

I surfaced about 20 yards out, keeping a rock between myself and the patrol boat. They spotted me from the guard bunker. I could see a Marine with his field glasses trained on me. I waved at him. One of the guards finally recognized me and waved back. Then the patrol boat got the message from the sergeant on the beach and took off. I climbed out of the water, quite shaken, but I didn't want to let on to the sergeant. I said to him, "Thanks for the gear. Nothing damaged. And, say, I hope you got that boat's license number." I took the equipment off as fast as I could and got out of there before the sergeant could get up a good head of steam. Several weeks passed before I could convince him to lend me his scuba gear again.

After two months in Chu Lai, I was getting restless and wanted to go to the front. The only time I had heard shots fired, except for the patrol boat incident, was when a drunk Marine sprayed the tree line with his machine gun. Then the

Army was flown in to replace us, and we were moved north. My orders were to join the First Marines, Third Battalion, Mike Company, and I was flown to Da Nang, a busier area than Chu Lai.

We spent a lot of time on night patrols and night ambushes. We were sniped at and booby-trapped but rarely saw the enemy, since in this area they were Viet Cong rather than the North Vietnamese Army. You couldn't tell if you did see one. You might pick out someone thinking he was a VC, but you had no way of knowing for sure. He'd have no uniform, no weapon on him and would claim to be a farmer. It was very frustrating.

Though we were in a combat zone now, we still had a beach, and I could swim even if I had no chance to scuba dive. It was a position named Hill 4, nicknamed "the Riviera," which included 200 yards of beach on the South China Sea. Since it was not a secure area, we set up machine guns on either end of the sandy stretch. It was a bare-ass beach like in the old days in the South Bronx, only instead of cops or Paragon Oil guards, we had Viet Cong interfering with our swims. Every once in a while a sniper would open up, and all the swimmers would climb out of the water and take up positions while our machine guns clattered away.

After four months in the Da Nang area, our unit was chosen to become part of the Ninth Marine Amphibious Brigade. We were stationed on ships near the DMZ, floating up and down the coast ready to react when we were needed. Landing by helicopters, assault boats or Amtracs (amphibious vehicles), we'd help out the South Vietnamese or the Army when they ran into heavy fighting. Once we secured the area, we'd go back to our ships and cruise the coast again.

Then all hell broke loose—the Tet Offensive began. In our area the North Vietnamese came down in division strength, taking village after village along the Qua Viet River and threatening Dong Ha, one of our major bases. Our battalion landed north of the mouth of the river, and we fought our way back through the villages. At the point where the river turned north toward North Vietnam, we took the village of Mai-Say-Tai East. We now had everything to the east of the river, while the North Vietnamese were on the west bank in Mai-Say-Tai West. Then we began island hopping along the river in our Amtracs, securing the islands.

As part of our job, we searched the island villages for Vietnamese deserters and draft dodgers. Never great admirers of the South Vietnamese Army, we Marines were now completely disgusted with them. When the Tet Offensive began, American forces had to take the brunt of it, because so many of the ARVN soldiers took off their uniforms, turned in their weapons and went back to their villages.

I used to get letters from home asking me what I thought about the antiwar movement. Actually I thought very little about it; I had too many other things on my mind, like trying to stay alive. Politics were irrelevant. They told us to take a village, and that's exactly what we did. Never mind the reason why. I functioned as a fighting man, which is what I was trained to be, so I felt useful. Back behind the lines or in the States, a Marine fulfilled no real purpose, so officers spent their time worrying about how well enlisted men shined their shoes. Out in the jungle, everything was filthy except our weapons. And no officer had to tell us to keep our weapons cleaned, because we knew our lives depended on them.

Of course, Marines constantly bitched. But we didn't often complain about the reasons for our being in Vietnam. Our gripes centered on such things as the fact the Army always had their beer supplies brought in by the planeload while the Marines' beer supply was always running out.

As far as I did think about it, however, I was becoming disillusioned. I had gone over there with the idea that I was doing the right thing by these people, but by now I realized that the ones who were supposed to be on our side didn't give a damn. We Marines often couldn't get basic PX supplies. But when I walked through the markets in Da Nang and other towns, I saw stuff that was obviously meant for our PXs on sale in the black market. Sometimes I thought, what good is all this? Mostly, though, I concentrated on shooting before the other fellow shot.

At this time I was a corporal, the senior squad leader in our platoon. So many in our unit had been wounded or killed that I had moved up fast.

In early March we prepared for a major assault on Mai-Say-Tai West, across the river from our position. All the NVA units the Marine sweeps had forced away from the coastal area had ended up in and around Mai-Say-Tai West. Our assault boats were called Mike boats and carried about a platoon of troops. But we also had larger boats of the same type, called Papa boats, used to carry tanks. The night before the attack, headquarters sent us two Marine Recon divers to check the depth of the river and find out if we could use the Papa boats on the assault.

Marine Recon was the elite of the corps. They never went in for the publicity of the Army's Green Berets or the Navy's SEALS, but we Marines knew they were something special —well-trained, willing to swim anywhere and assault anything, totally gung-ho.

Late on a moonless night, the two divers prepared to enter the river along the section of the bank that my squad was guarding. I watched them as they donned their scuba gear, thinking of myself as a colleague, a fellow diver. I didn't realize until later just how much more advanced and better trained they were as divers than I.

They slipped silently into the water, and we heard nothing for a while. Then suddenly there were muffled booms, underwater explosions. A couple of Marines next to my position spotted a small fishing boat; NVA were in it, dropping grenades on the divers. We opened fire and drove the boat off. After several tense minutes, both Recon divers made it back to my position. How they did it, I don't know, because one was badly hurt. We couldn't put on a flashlight, but I could see he was bleeding from his ears. The concussion had probably ruptured his eardrums.

My adrenaline was pumping now and, without thinking, I decided I'd give the guys a hand. I went up to the Recon sergeant and said, "Hey, I'm a diver myself. I can take over for your buddy."

"Forget it," he told me. "Just stay where you are." After seeing that his buddy was being taken care of, he headed back into the water. I stood there watching.

Now that the idea had entered my head, I had to do it. The wounded diver's gear was lying there. No one was watching. I checked the regulator. It worked. I put the compass on my wrist, then put on the fins, the mask and the tank. I put on the regulator mouthpiece in my mouth and waded into the water.

I knew what I was going to do. While the sergeant was checking depths near the hostile village on the west bank, I'd check out the depths closer to our area where the river bent toward the sea. When I came back I'd walk up to the Recon diver and say, "Sergeant, I thought I might help out anyway, and here're the depth readings."

I had never done a night dive, but I wasn't worried. All I had to do was follow the bottom of the river out to the middle, then come back. I couldn't get lost out there because I had the wounded diver's compass.

It was so dark in that water I could feel the blackness as well as see it. But it was okay. I moved slowly, easily, touching the bottom with my hand and glancing at the illuminated numbers on the depth gauge. I figured I must be near the middle now. I looked at the depth gauge once more and turned around. I thought I was heading back the way I came, but I had moved around enough by now that I wasn't at all sure which direction was home. No reason to get scared, I told myself. No problem. I checked the compass. I checked it again. The needle was locked! The damn thing was busted —must have been damaged by the grenade blasts! Why the hell hadn't I noticed that before?

I was scared now, as close to sheer terror as I'd ever been. I was swallowed in pitch blackness, lost on the bottom of a river, with the North Vietnamese up there somewhere. My first night dive, and I had to pick this place to do it. I had no business trying to match the Recon divers. This was their job, not mine. Wait a minute now, I told myself. Breathe easier. You'll get back. Just think a minute. I knew I had to get a grip on myself—all those bubbles from my frantic breathing might attract attention.

I decided the only thing to do was feel my way along the bottom, following the contours toward shallower water. I was disoriented and could only guess which bank I was heading for, but it was getting shallower. Alright, you've almost made it. I kept below water as long as I could, then stuck my head up.

It turned out to be a sandbar in no-man's land, about 40 yards across from my position. No one except the Marines in my foxhole and the next one over knew I was out there. I climbed on the sandbar, keeping low, feeling sure some Marine would open up if he saw me. To hell with proper military procedure—I started yelling, "Hey, it's me, Gott, don't shoot." I'd never get back if I dove under again. It was too black down there. I began swimming back on the surface.

When I got within 20 yards, the sky suddenly was lit by flares. We hadn't been using them while the Recon divers were in, but apparently the Recon sergeant must have reported back. Any second I would be spotted and someone would start blasting. "It's me . . . Gott . . . Don't shoot . . . U.S. Marines . . . New York Mets . . . Babe Ruth." Then

I heard laughing. "What the hell you doing out there, Gott? Taking a bath? You sure make an ugly fish, boy."

I relaxed and climbed up the bank. Now the only thing I had to worry about was getting into trouble for my unauthorized mission. If the Recon sergeant complained to my lieutenant, I'd be in hot water. The sergeant turned out to be a good guy, though. He was only concerned with his buddy and didn't care that I had endangered his buddy's equipment. No one reported me.

I settled down to sleep for a few hours. I felt foolish, I'd overestimated my diving ability and could have gotten myself killed as a result. Someday, I promised myself, I'd really learn to be a good diver. But I didn't dwell on it too long, because I had other things on my mind.

The next morning we made our assault. We knew it would be rough. The North Vietnamese were tough soldiers, who could be expected to stand and fight—and at Mai-Say-Tai West, that's what they did.

I wasn't in the battle very long. The front ramp on the Mike boat dropped, and my platoon charged out toward the village. We were taking heavy incoming fire. Four of us charged a hooch from which someone was firing at us. We went in the front door, firing, and a North Vietnamese soldier went out the back door, throwing behind a hand grenade. I saw the flash and felt the explosion burning shrapnel into me.

Three of the four of us were hit. I called up a resupply vehicle and it came up to the house and took us back across the river. I could walk, but I had taken some shrapnel in one foot and was limping. To help myself along as I got out of the vehicle, I used my rifle as a crutch—and bayonetted myself in the other foot. I felt like an idiot, especially since I pulled that stunt in front of both my colonel and major who'd come over to ask me how things were going.

While waiting with the other injured for the medivac helicopter, I checked myself over and decided that I wasn't in too bad a shape. The grenade explosion had been hot enough to cauterize my wounds and I wasn't bleeding badly, nor did I feel much pain. When the corpsman came to administer morphine, I refused it, not noticing that he had already put a "morphine administered" tag on me. The helicopter ride was fast, windy and cold, very cold.

I was brought into a noncritical operating ward at Dong Ha. Two Air Force doctors looked me over, then began prying pieces of shrapnel out of me with forceps. I yelled from the pain and told them I hadn't had any morphine, but they wouldn't believe me. Wounded Marine, must be raving, delirious. So they waited five minutes for the morphine to take effect, then came back and began digging at a piece of shrapnel in my right elbow. I yelled bloody murder. Up to this point, I'd very proudly remained calm about my injury. But now I began working up a strong antagonism to one of the doctors, a rear-force commando type with a pearl-handled pistol slung low around his hips. To scare him into giving me the morphine, I reached for the doc's pistol with my left hand. I got my hand on it, and he grabbed for it. The two of us fought a tug-of-war, but he finally won. He did decide to give me some Demerol, however.

That made everything all right again. I merrily floated in my own world as they pulled out shrapnel, inserted drains and bandaged me up. Two hours later I was flown to a hospital in Da Nang, where I had the first fresh milk I'd drunk in a year. The following day, I was moved again, this time to Cam Rahn Bay.

Soldiers in Cam Rahn Bay walked around in clean uniforms, with shined boots and no guns in sight. The base had long been totally insulated from the war. That night, lying in the hospital ward, I heard explosions. I hobbled into the shower room, which I knew was well protected by concrete tile walls. A woman lieutenant colonel yelled to the nurse, "Turn off the lights, we're under attack." The nurse replied, "Oh no, we're *never* under attack." When she finally began herding people into the shower room, she was surprised to find me already there. "What are you doing here?" she asked. "Just keeping a few steps ahead," I said.

After two days at Cam Rahn Bay, I was flown home on a giant C-141 transport. Being spaced out on some drug, I didn't notice that when they unloaded some of the wounded in Japan my bag of personal belongings was also unloaded. Not only did I lose my wallet, but also a pair of tanker's goggles I'd won in a card game, a set of NVA lieutenant's bars I'd gotten in the war and maps that had helped me survive the war. I knew that some orderly who'd never gotten closer to Vietnam than Japan would now be using my souvenirs to tell his war stories.

We landed in Alaska, then at Andrews Air Force Base outside Baltimore, where we stayed for the night. The next day I arrived at Floyd Bennett Airfield in New York to be taken to St. Alban's Hospital in Brooklyn. When they carried us off the plane on stretchers—I could have walked but they insisted I had to be carried—they put us on a runway to wait for the ambulances. It was snowing. I hadn't seen snow in a long time, and it looked good. I opened my blankets to let it fall on me. The medical officer looked at me like I was crazy, but he hadn't spent a year in Vietnam.

CHAPTER 4

THE MEDITERRANEAN, THE IONIAN, THE AEGEAN

In *Life and Death in the Coral Sea,* Jacques Cousteau wrote "In theory, we know that the sea and the bottom are very different from one region to another; but what makes the sea such a marvelous adventure is that it is really impossible to imagine, unless we have actually seen it, to what extent it differs from one place to the next."

Thanks to the Marines, I enjoyed the "marvelous adventure" of experiencing some of that variety before I was 21. First it had been a taste of West Coast diving, then my less-then-pleasant Vietnam dives. Now, however, in the summer of 1968, I was assigned to a Mediterranean cruise. I'd see Spain, France, Italy, Greece and Turkey. I'd walk among the ruins of the ancient civilizations I had enjoyed reading about in my history courses. But it wasn't just the countries that excited me—it was the Mediterranean itself. Over its waters, the ships of the Phoenicians and Greeks had sailed; beneath its waters, wrecks of these ancient ships and even ancient cities now lay.

Off Marseilles, Cousteau once discovered a Roman ship, containing amphorae, earthenware vases in which the ancients carried their cargo. Cousteau and his crew found one intact, with wine sloshing around inside; they opened it and drank 2200-year-old wine.

I had read about Caesara, a port city built by the Romans

in 10 B.C., which now lies off Israel's coast and can be visited by scuba divers. In the Aegean Sea off the island of Melos, the walls of the ancient city of Emborium can be seen. Twelve years before my cruise two young Greek snorklers spotted part of a large Ionic column in 25 feet of water off the Peloponnesian coast. It turned out to be the lost city of Pheia, mentioned by Homer. An earthquake had dumped it into the bay in ancient times.

Perhaps other cities beneath the waves still awaited discoverers. Maybe Atlantis was in the Mediterranean—and I'd be the diver to find it.

I had another reason for wanting to go to the Mediterranean. I hadn't liked Marine life in the States from the very first minute I returned to duty. After spending a month in St. Alban's Hospital, I reported to the Brooklyn Navy Yard for reassignment, wearing utilities ("fatigues" in Army terminology) and penny loafers.

"Corporal, what do you mean coming in here dressed like that?" a lieutenant screamed at me as soon as I walked into the office. He looked as if he'd been sitting there all morning waiting for something to go wrong so he could let off steam. I explained that I didn't have any uniforms, my sea bag not having caught up with me yet. That got *me* off the hook, but then he asked, "Do you mean the corporal over at the hospital didn't see to it that your were properly uniformed before you came here?" He needed someone to get mad at.

It was like that for the next few months: white glove inspections, officers worrying about shoe shines, floors to scrub and scrub again. The Marine Corps trained men to fight and didn't seem to know what to do with us when we weren't fighting, except keep us busy with petty nonsense. Mediterranean duty, I was told, involved less hassle, was a little looser than stateside duty.

When I saw the ship I was assigned to, I was a little less

excited by the trip. It was a raggedy old APA, a troop carrier that could have dated back to the Mexican–American war, judging by its looks. I couldn't bring scuba gear with me since, unlike the Navy crewmen, we had no storage space except for our sea bags, not even a small locker. I did manage, however, to fit mask, snorkle and fins into my bag.

On the way across the Atlantic, I talked about diving with the sailors as well as the Marines. Finally I met a sailor, Brad, who had diving equipment stashed away in his locker. Brad was a pinochle player, and I began to join in his games. And I didn't push too hard to win every game.

"I hear there's some good diving off Spain, Brad. Ever dive there?"

"Yeah."

"Plan on doing any diving this time?"

"Maybe, I don't know."

"I sure as hell wish I could have brought my scuba gear along."

But Brad made no offers to lend me his, and I didn't want to push too hard right away.

Our first port was Rota, Spain, headquarters of the Sixth Fleet. Rota lies on the Atlantic coast of Spain, and I soon found an ocean beach I liked. Snorkling far out from shore, I saw out of the corner of my eye some large shapes swimming rapidly toward me. For a second, I was startled, thinking they might be sharks. But then I saw the bottle noses and the smiling mouths, and I relaxed. Sharks never smile, but the dolphins' permanent smiling expression symbolizes their friendliness.

The dolphins seemed to be very curious about me and wanted to find out what kind of playmate I'd make. I was a little nervous at first, swimming among what must have been a hundred playful mammals. I worried they might accidentally hurt me. But after they did their acrobatics a few times —high speed leaps, plunges and turns—I realized that they weren't going to ram me, even though they kept racing up to me from behind, beneath, every angle, and turning away at the last moment. They never even bumped into each other.

They would swim in a straight line, turn on a dime and be swimming back in the opposite direction in the time it took me to turn my head. I wondered if I could pet one. I extended my hand, palm out, and a dolphin swam along it, brushing its skin against my hand. It seemed to like it, for it turned around and immediately came back for another petting.

I tired of playing with the dolphins long before they tired of playing with me. They didn't seem to want me to leave when I started swimming for the shore.

I've been fascinated with dolphins since that encounter. But I've never been able to reestablish my friendship. Once, on a diving trip off Spanish Honduras, dolphins suddenly appeared all around our boat. My diving buddy Bill Whalen and I grabbed our scuba gear, put it on as fast as we could and made a quick exit off the back of the boat. But just when we hit the water, they all disappeared.

Most encounters with dolphins are that way, but, as I had found out, once in a while they show an eagerness to play with humans. More than that, though, a dolphin has never been known to attack a human, not in self defense nor even when a man steals a baby dolphin from its mother. The ancient Greeks had myths about dolphins saving drowning sailors, letting them ride on their backs and bringing them to shore. In modern times we have many documented cases of dolphins befriending and aiding humans in one way or another.

This friendly attitude of dolphins toward humans is a puzzle. Some species of dolphins take to captivity well and can easily be trained as water circus performers, but the ocean roaming dolphins presumedly have had little or no contact with humans. We've done nothing for them, haven't fed them or protected them in any way. And yet they like us.

Dolphins are interesting creatures in their own right, too. Air-breathing, warm-blooded mammals, dolphins evolved millions of years ago from land animals. They make love and raise their children in ways similar to ours. They see underwater better than we do, but they navigate more by sonar than vision. Those constant squeaks dolphins make aren't idle chatter; they enable dolphins to identify objects at greater distances than we can with our eyes above water. Dolphins have brains as large as ours and have long been believed to be among the most intelligent of mammals. Experiments have demonstrated at least the possibility that dolphins have their own language. Despite their meekness toward humans, dolphins fight other predators very successfully. They can even kill sharks by ramming them with their noses.

Our afloat group sailed from Rota through the Straits of Gibraltar, and there they were again—dolphins by the thousands. It almost looked as if I could jump off the ship and walk to Africa or Europe on their backs. They raced the ship and frolicked around it. For some reason, dolphins often pass between the Atlantic and the Mediterranean, and this day the Straits teemed with them. I was pleased to see them again.

One of our group's assignments was to take part in a military exercise with Greek and British forces. We took the role of an invading force that would land in western Greece, from the Ionian Sea, and push into the mountains, there to be met by the Greek and British. It didn't quite work out that way, though.

At three o'clock in the morning we climbed down nets from the ship onto the Amtracs, then rode around in circles until receiving the signal from the flagship to head in. When the Amtrac pulled up to the beach and dropped its front ramp, we charged out. The beach was occupied by a local couple who thought they had it to themselves that night. A blond woman, carrying stray items of clothing, bounded up the beach ahead of us followed by her boyfriend, much to the delight of the invaders.

We were supposed to coordinate on the beach, then head into the mountains. We never made it. We got pinned down by the local civilians. As soon as the sun rose, people began pouring out of the village to our right, with carts loaded down with wine and grapes, watermelons, bread and cheese. They came among us playing bouzoukis and accordians, dancing and passing around bottles of ouzo. Let the brass worry about their big time military operation, we Marines were having a fine time where we were.

As soon as it became obvious that our unexpected reception had thrown off the whole schedule, the operation was scratched. While the high command was making up its mind what to do with us, we stayed on the beach living in tents, doing nothing. Beer and other essentials were shipped in by supply boat. My tent was near the water. I could sit on a low cliff and watch the dark blue but clear water below, rolling in and breaking on the rocks. It was beautiful, this Ionian Sea.

Before the operation, Brad had finally promised to let me borrow his scuba gear as soon as we got a chance. Now was the chance. I found a sailor on a supply boat and asked him to give Brad a message: Water's beautiful, send me the scuba. But the supply boats' chief petty officer refused to bring in the tanks. Brad did, however, succeed in sending in my mask, fins and snorkle.

The rocky coast was honeycombed with coves and inlets of every size. I explored all the nearby ones, enjoying the various shapes the rocks had been formed into, above and below the surface of the water. Life was pleasant. By night, I'd drink and dance with the Greeks—all men, they didn't allow their women to attend our parties. By day, I'd snorkle and dive in the Ionian Sea.

I decided that it would be nice to have some fresh fish for

dinner. From an old inner tube I made a hand sling, and I whittled some spears from tree branches. I'd like to report that we began enjoying a nightly fish fry, but it didn't happen. Sea life wasn't very plentiful. And each time I did find a fish, and managed to sling the spear accurately enough, the spear bounced off. I still had a long way to go as a spear fisherman.

After eight days on the beach, we were finally loaded back on the ships. Normally, the conclusion of a military exercise is good news. But I hated to see this one end.

The people of Malta did not like us as much as the Greeks did. But I didn't find that out until after I'd been scuba diving in their waters.

I took a bus tour of the island with three buddies, and after growing bored with churches, we left the tour, had a few drinks in a local bar, then took a taxi back. On the way I noticed a cove with buildings going down to the water. I liked the look of it and thought it might make an interesting dive.

The next day I borrowed Brad's gear. Brad and I were good friends now, and he let me borrow the equipment whenever he wasn't using it himself.

Rick Neimeyer, a Navy corpsman I'd become friendly with, wanted to come along with me, though he didn't dive. We got to the cove and went to the edge of a short, rocky beach. While I put on my gear, I explained to Rick each piece's function. I offered to give him a try with it, but he said he'd rather sit on the beach. He opened a flask of Scotch and wished me luck.

In 30 feet of clear blue water, I floated into a jumble of ruins: foundations, archways, columns. It could have been the remains of a sunken city of antiquity. I imagined a thriving Greek city. Among these columns, many centuries ago, philosophers, soldiers and dramatists strolled and craftsmen hawked their wares in an open air market. Now the market had become rubble, the air had become water, and the very city itself was lost.

That was the daydream the scene conjured. I was actually seeing foundations of the buildings at the water's edge, concrete underwater moorings, the stones and rubble of modern civilization tumbled into the harbor by natural disasters or perhaps by the bombings of World War II. The way the light filtered through the water made it all look as magic as an ancient city.

Malta must not have had many scuba divers. My entrance into the water had attracted a number of people who then wandered over, waiting to see if I'd emerge. When I came out, Rick was talking to three women, explaining what scuba diving was all about. The women were British, and after chatting for a while, we arranged to meet them for dinner later on. That's one thing about scuba diving: It provides an easy way to meet people. Rick found that out without even bothering to dive.

The next night I had Shore Patrol duty and wound up in the heaviest action I'd seen since Vietnam. A lieutenant and I were called to a bar where a fight had broken out. The trouble had started between a Marine and a bartender, and when the fighting began, all the Marines joined together and started knocking down everyone else, as they are trained to do. When I arrived, it was raging hot and heavy between the Marines and the locals.

A Marine saw my Shore Patrol armband and came at me with a broken wine bottle. "Hey, man, knock it off," I said. "I'm a Marine, too. I don't want to lock anyone up. I just want to get you guys out of here." He looked at me, then at the bottle in his hand, and said, "Yeah, I guess you're right," and walked out.

By that time, the fighting had spread to the street known as Pig Alley, which was lined with bars for a dozen blocks.

The Maltese must have been bearing some grudge against the American military. Crowds of them were wandering the streets, throwing rocks and attacking Marines and sailors in the area, who were fighting back. The militia were quickly called out, but that didn't help us since they just clubbed away at American uniforms instead of trying to separate the two groups.

I tried to round up sailors and Marines and get them headed back to the ships. Then I found myself trapped in a bar with an angry crowd outside and the owner had to shut his gates to prevent them from getting in at me. I decided that my best move would be to get back to the ship myself. I almost made it, but I had to run through a square into which several hundred civilians were pouring from two side streets, converging on a group of 80 or so Americans at the far end. I heard shots and ran a little faster. Then som one hit me on the calf with a cobblestone and down I went. I kicked myself clear of a man swinging a chair at me, and joined our group, limping badly.

We were all heading back for the ship when an old salt of a gunnery sergeant boomed out a short, inspirational message about not taking no crap from nobody. He turned the group around, and even though they were heavily outnumbered, they marched back into the fray. But I was already wounded and continued on to the dock, where I joined dozens of other injured sailors and Marines being given first aid. While they loaded us onto stretchers to send us back to our ships, everyone was loudly recounting his tales; most seemed to have had a good time that night.

Our admirals decided to put together a war game and sailed us off to Sardinia. I missed this exercise, though. Since my left leg was bruised and swollen and my calf muscles knotted like a rock, I could barely walk. I stayed aboard and played pinochle while everyone else ran up and down hills.

The afloat group made one of its stops at Izmir, Turkey, which is located on a bay off the Aegean Sea. Returning from the Trojan War, Ulysses lost his way on the Aegean and had many wonderful adventures—or so Homer tells us. One adventure he didn't have that I planned on was exploring beneath the surface of that sea.

Carrying Brad's scuba, Rick and I caught a taxi in Izmir, a busy city, and told the driver to head along the coast road. We ran up quite a bill by the time we found a lovely, isolated cove. A few miles outside of Izmir, a different world exists, a different era of history. The only people around, after we paid the puzzled taxi driver, were shepherds on the grassy slopes that led into the mountains. They watched with great curiosity as I donned the gear and waded in. Their world seemed strange to me, but to them I must have looked as if I were literally from another world.

In the deep blue waters, I found creatures that Homer would have loved to write about, if only he'd known. As I swam along the bottom, I saw ahead of me what looked like a meadow with thick stalks of grass rising from the sandy bottom, gently waving in the current. As I swam closer, the stalks receded into the sand. I swam over the field, and it was like a wave: The ones closest to me had disappeared all the way into the sand, the ones a little farther away only partly, while the ones still farther remained at full length, waving like cobras. I looked behind me and saw that they seemed to be growing back as I passed. It was like a speeded-up sequence showing the growth of plants in a Walt Disney nature film. I knew these weren't plants, though, since I could see their eyes and mouths.

Later I found out that they were a type of eel, called garden eels. They have permanent homes on the bottom which they never leave. They can extend themselves out or, as I saw, withdraw into their holes. Normally, they face the current, feeding on whatever happens by.

I returned to the States in February 1969. A few weeks later I was standing in the morning formation when the colonel came over to my company and called out several names, including mine. I thought, oh my God, now I must be in some kind of big trouble. I marched forward and the captain, standing next to the colonel, laid sergeant's chevrons in my hand. That was a surprise; I hadn't realized I was in line for a promotion.

But a more pleasant surprise came two weeks later. The president had announced an "early out" program. If you'd served overseas and had less than six months left in service, you could get out immediately. Sergeant's chevrons or not, I opted out. Nothing the company "career advisor" said could change my mind. I flew back to New York in April of 1969.

After two and a half years as a Marine, I was a free man, and I liked the feeling. I relaxed for the first few months. I had the summer, and I had scuba diving. Now I could dive when and where I wanted, with my own equipment.

Beneath the surface of the sea, I had no officers and no enemies. No one worried me about my shoe shines; no one wanted to shoot me or to throw a brick at me. With almost no exceptions, nothing that lived in the sea would bother me if I didn't bother it. Down there I could be free and at peace with the world.

That was the kind of marine life I wanted.

CHAPTER 5

TO SPEAR OR NOT TO SPEAR

Scuba is something more than a sport, a hobby or a leisure activity. It's a vehicle into a new world that offers a multitude of possibilities to each diver: exploring a new landscape, wreck diving, underwater photography, spearfishing, shell or bottle collecting or cave diving.

After leaving the Marines in April 1969, the first underwater activity I concentrated on was spearfishing. My reason was very basic: Nothing tastes better to me than freshly caught fish.

Though it took me many years to progress to a level of competence, I had begun spearfishing in my early teens. My first spear was a car aerial, which were plentiful in the Bronx. I bent the tip over, filed a point on it and used it to hand spear the monsters of the deep—without much success. When I was 14, I bought a Hawaiian sling, a hollow wooden tube with a shaft in it and a rubber loop at one end. The shaft is drawn back against the loop, then released. In my hands, it was a very sporting weapon. I managed to bruise a number of fish, but rarely killed any.

By the summer of '69, I was using a hand spear for fluke and flounder, two bottom fish that are among my favorite dishes. But the blackfish (tautog) was what I most wanted as a quarry, because that's the seafood I like best of all. They were too quick for a hand spear, so a friend gave me a light, small bandgun, a pistol-handled contraption powered by two strands of rubber tubing. I was eager to try it, and my next time in the water I sneaked up to a blackfish and fired. The shaft bounced off the fish's head.

I bought a more powerful bandgun and decided to learn more about the sport of spearfishing. I read all the books and asked my fellow divers all sorts of questions. Mostly, though, I learned by experience.

When I saw that a blackfish was spooked when approached from one particular angle, I'd remember and try another angle. After a number of years now, my technique with blackfish is well developed. First, I know their habitat. They live near rocks or pilings, because they feed on the shellfish—mussels, crabs and barnacles—that live there. I snorkle on the surface in these areas. When I spot one, I dive away from the fish, go deeper, then come up from slightly below and behind, where it can't see me. If I don't spook the blackfish, I try to get within three or four feet before firing, aiming for just behind the gill plates. If it spooks, I'll back off slightly and stay around. A blackfish makes its home in a specific area, and even when it is scared off, it will return to that area very shortly.

I've never been interested in spearing fish for the sake of their size or reputation as a game fish—or for the thrill of it. I learned early, from my father, to respect nature and its creatures. When my family was out on a picnic and a bee landed on the table, no one would pick up a newspaper and swat it. My father had taught us that the bee had a right to live. If you wanted to kill something, you should have a damn good reason to do so. From my earliest attempts, therefore, I never killed a fish I didn't intend to eat.

The largest fish I ever speared was a 21-pound fluke. I had my bandgun, since I was after blackfish, and I spotted it rising off the bottom in poor visibility. As it disappeared into a mud cloud four feet away, I just guessed at its location and fired. I knew I had guessed right, because the gun was almost torn out of my hands. For me, the pleasure of having shot a 21-pounder came from the fact that I had so much more fish to eat.

I like to eat lobster, too, especially the clawed North American variety. "Bugs," as divers call them, are caught by hand. The first time I tried to grab one, it grabbed me first. But lobster tastes too good, and is too expensive in fish markets, not to learn the techniques of lobster catching quickly. Lobsters are usually found in holes or under rocks, with the antennae or claws showing. A diver with fast hands should grab both claws, not just one because the other claw will quickly find the diver's hand. The legs or antennae shouldn't be grabbed because they break off. Even the claws sometimes separate from the body of the lobster. The best place to grab the lobster—if you can reach it or after you've pulled it out of its hole—is under the body. And the main rule to follow is to seize it quickly before it has a chance to seize you.

Recently, controversy has heated up in diving circles over spearfishing, whether it should be done with scuba gear, what weapons should be used, or whether it should be banned entirely. Jacques Cousteau has condemned it, and his company, U.S. Divers, stopped making spearguns. Hans Hass, an early spearfishing enthusiast who never used anything but a pole spear, has also condemned all spearfishing. Many countries prohibit spearfishing using scuba. This controversy is healthy, I believe, because it can lead to a better appreciation of the proper role of humans in the marine world. I know that, over the years, my attitudes toward the sport went through an evolution as my spearfishing proficiency increased.

Part of the reason for the outcry against the sport is that

The claws of this II-pound lobster weren't tied when Bill Gleason grabbed it. (*Photo by Don Arrington*)

it has seemingly depopulated many reefs of marine life. Spearfishing may not actually kill off all the fish, but it can have the same effect. On many tropical reefs where colorful fish would once swim up to scuba divers or ignore them, spearfishing has turned these fish gun-shy. When a diver enters the water, the fish quickly disappear, having learned that a diving human is an enemy. Spearfishing a reef, therefore, interferes with other scuba divers' enjoyment.

Also damaging to spearfishing's reputation have been competitions in the sport. The winners are those who kill the most and the biggest fish. At the end of the competition, beaches are often filled with dead fish that no one really wants to eat.

I agree with many of the complaints against spearfishing, but I can't accept the argument that all spearfishing is wrong. It seems to me that no one but a strict vegetarian should maintain that position.

Spearfishing certainly isn't to blame for very many of the ocean's ecology problems. One trawler can catch more fish in one day than all the world's spearfishermen could catch in a month. And pollution does far more damage to marine life in coastal areas than does spearfishing.

To me, spearfishing is a proper sport if the spearfisherman accepts certain limitations which give the prey a chance to escape, and if he only seeks food for his table. It's not enough just for the spearfisherman to hope someone will eat the fish he kills. Everyone who has done any fishing knows that the fish he generously gives to his neighbors, because he has caught more than he can use, often gets thrown out. And that's wrong. To avoid becoming despoilers of the undersea world, the spearfisherman must do more than just respect the local fish and game laws. These laws don't cover all the situations a conservation-minded spearfisherman encounters.

For example, once I was hunting for blackfish with little

luck. Then one came within range. It looked small, maybe not quite big enough for a meal in itself, but I decided to spear it. I'd probably spear another before I finished diving for the day, and between the two of them I'd get a meal. I didn't get the second blackfish, though. Back on the beach I took a close look at my one prey, and the amount of meat I knew I'd get off it just didn't seem worth the time and effort of gutting, cleaning, filleting and cooking it. I remember sitting on a rock, staring at the fish, torn between throwing it away and going to all that trouble for a few bites. I finally did eat the fish, knowing I should since I had killed it, but I made up my mind that I would never again shoot anything that wasn't big enough to make a meal in itself.

I also decided never to go beyond rubber-powered spears in my underwater hunting. More sophisticated and high-powered spearguns, operated by compressed air or CO_2 gas, are on the market. But these guns upset the balance between prey and predator too greatly. I believe that the fish should have a chance to escape its human predator. To deserve his meal, the spearfisherman should be clever and cunning enough to come out the winner in a contest and not just blast the fish out of the water.

Several years ago, I spearfished wearing scuba gear. Now the only time I wear tanks spearfishing is when I'm going after bottom fish beyond my free diving range. In all other circumstances, I spearfish only by free diving. (Terms vary, but by free diving I mean diving without tanks, what is commonly called skin diving.)

Free diving is really a different sport than scuba, though the basics of it are taught in scuba courses. It demands more of the diver physically, and it requires a different set of techniques for the free diver to enter the underwater world sleekly, without waste effort. Free diving isn't always associated with spearfishing, but that often provides the motive for it.

These days, I do most of my spearfishing off Newport, Rhode Island, with Carl Miller, a fellow instructor at the Skin Diving School of New York. Carl is one of the finest spearfishermen I've ever seen, and I've learned a lot about the sport from him. Often Carl and I and one or two other instructors go up to Newport with our inflatable boats and spend the whole weekend without putting on tanks. We usually head for Brenton Reef or Seal Rock in the open ocean south of Newport and spearfish for blackfish or strippers. Each boat has one buddy-team. If the current is running, one buddy spearfishes while the other stays in the boat, ready to maneuver to pick up the one in the water. When currents present no problems, both buddies will be in the water at the same time. Both of them snorkle on the surface looking for fish and take turns going down for a shot. Both shouldn't be underwater together because if one then gets into trouble the other won't have enough air to go to his aid. The buddy watching from the top can take a full breath if it looks as if he's needed below. I'll usually dive 15 or 20 feet; most fish can be found in that depth. I can reach 40 feet if I have to but I then find it hard to stay down there long enough to spear a fish. Those aren't very impressive figures. Greek sponge divers regularly work below 150 feet without air, as do the women pearl divers of Japan. The current free-diving record is 240 feet, held by a diver named Robert Croft.

As a safety precaution, we never carry our stringers of fish hanging from our belts. We leave them dangling from the boat. Dying fish can attract sharks, and I don't want my hip connected with the stringer in case the shark has a large bite.

Free diving illustrates the respect for the ocean environment and its inhabitants which should guide the spear fisherman. When a diver becomes a predator, he must do it on the ocean's terms, not human terms. He must kill not for the sake of killing—humans are the only creatures who do that

—but for the sake of a meal. And by accepting certain limitations on the use of air and weaponry, the spearfisherman becomes more like a normal marine predator than a destroyer. If he uses advanced technology to kill fish without limits, just for the thrill of it, he becomes an enemy not only to marine creatures but to every diver who loves the underwater world.

Because all of us have this dangerously destructive instinct we must learn to control, I try to help my divers develop appreciation for the underwater environment they're about to enter. If I ever catch them killing marine life without the intention of eating it, I tell them they are out of the class. Every living thing down there is part of a food cycle, even conches and coral. The only excuse you have to kill any of it is if you enter into the life cycle and eat what you kill.

I want my students to stop thinking as humans; that's dangerous to the ocean. I want each one of them to think as an amphibian—a life form that kills only to eat.

When I returned home from the Marines, I'd had enough diving experience to know that I had much more to learn, and I wanted to become a first-rate diver. To buy my equipment, I went to Cougar Sports, a pro dive and pro archery shop in the northern Bronx. Cougar has a policy of not selling breathing equipment to uncertified divers, so I signed up for the basic certification course at the Skin Diving School of New York, a National Association of Skin Diving Schools program run out of Cougar. The course was easy enough for me, but I still learned from it. And I went on to take the advanced open water course that fall.

Like many pro dive shops, Cougar is a gathering place for divers. I went on wreck dives with the people I met there and began making the shop my home away from home. From the spring until the fall, I spent almost all of my free time diving. The non-free time I spent trying to make a living.

While I was in the Marines, I'd done absolutely no thinking about my future. When I again found myself a civilian, I went to the government employment agency, and they laid out a number of possibilities. None of them sounded interesting.

The first interview I went on was for an insurance job. I didn't really think I wanted to be an insurance salesman, so I made what seemed to me to be an outrageous salary demand. They were impressed with my ambition and hired me. After going to insurance school, earning my license and beginning to sell, I decided it wasn't for me. After four months, I quit.

My father kept telling me to take civil service exams, so I took almost every one that came along for a while. But when the Fire Department wrote to ask me to come in for an interview, I decided I didn't want to be a fireman. When the Border Patrol called, I decided I didn't want to be a border patrolman. I felt no desire to plunge into any kind of career. I lived at home with my parents and I had saved some money from the Marines. For all the nonsense I'd put up with in the Corps, I'd had some real experiences there that made ordinary job concerns seem petty. Security didn't interest me much. If I wanted that, I could have stayed in the service.

The next job I tried was in construction. That lasted a month. My foreman and I disagreed on my job definition. I thought I was hired as a construction worker, and he thought I was hired to run back and forth to the bar across the street —to buy him six-packs.

Between jobs, I worked at Bronx Fordham service station for John Hilbert. I liked the job, since John, who is a close friend today, never minded if I took off to go diving on a sunny day. But I could hardly call it a career. Eventually I began thinking I should find something long-term. By the time the Corrections Department wrote to me, I was ready again to try something, even though I'd already let better civil service jobs pass by.

I should have known better. It was too much like the worst part of the Marines. After nine months of hassle, the final straw came as I was sitting at the main gate of a prison. The sergeant in the building across from the gate called me up to tell me, "You're out of uniform. Put your hat on." I decided right then to quit. Once again I didn't bother finding another job before I did.

I didn't really want another job then. It was July, and my friends and I still had nearly two months left on the summer house we had rented in the Hamptons on the eastern end of Long Island. I moved out there for the rest of the summer, while the other five came out mostly on weekends.

I was known as Aquaman around the house because I was the only diver in the group. I kept a different schedule from the others. On weekends we'd all be out partying until three or four in the morning. I'd then sleep for a couple of hours, get up at seven, put my equipment in the car and head for the water. I'd return at ten or eleven, clean and fillet the fish I generally brought back with me, and then catch up on my sleep in the afternoon.

I didn't mind that the others didn't dive; I could always find someone to dive with. Eastern Long Island is a great area for divers. It doesn't have the colorful coral reefs or the clear water of the Caribbean, but it does have a fine and varied shoreline: sandy ocean beaches, rocky jetties, inlets, calm bays and challenging ocean currents. What makes the area so good for diving, however, is the abundance of sea life. The waters teem with fish of all kinds: fluke and flounder, blackfish and bluefish, porgy and pollack, sturgeon and sunfish, stripers and—sharks. The novel (though not the movie) *Jaws* is set in Eastern Long Island, for a reason. It is a good fishing area, and sharks fish where men do.

I met my first shark out there in the summer of '69, diving

under the Shinnecock Inlet Bridge which is a prime fishing area. The shark looked huge, but my buddy and I both controlled the impulse to buzz off. Instead we hugged the ground, then slowly backed out. The shark seemed curious about us but didn't pursue us.

More dangerous was a school of bluefish I met in the same Shinnecock Inlet area, where I mostly dived. My buddy and I were just leaving the water after a spearfishing dive when the whole surface exploded with ripples and fish. I heard a fisherman on the beach say that they were top mackerel. I knew that a school of bluefish must be close behind, feeding on them and forcing them to the surface. We still had air in our tanks so I said to my buddy, "Let's go back in and take a look."

I didn't bother with my speargun, since I don't care for the taste of bluefish. When I got underwater all I could see were top mackerel jumping all around me. Then I saw a mass of bluefish. I have never seen so many fish in my life. It was like running up against a brick wall. They were feeding, and when blues feed they aren't fussy. Fishermen know to be wary of the bite of a bluefish, even when it has been landed, and here I was in the middle of hundreds of them. With their sharp teeth, they bit at my fins, my wet suit and my regulator hose. The two of us got out of the way of that school as fast as we could, before they did any serious damage to us or our equipment.

The summer that I quit my Corrections Department job, I met a man who started me thinking about my future. I was getting into my wet suit near Shinnecock Inlet, when a diver came over looking for a spearfishing buddy. We teamed up and had a good dive, spearing some fluke. After we got out of our wet suits, he invited me back to his camper for dinner. I drove into town to buy some wine, and his wife had the fish sizzling away by the time I got back.

Bill Whalen, Bill Gleason and I display some blackfish and stripers we just speared off Newport. *(Photo by Terry Conmy)*

After dinner we sat around and talked. It turned out that he had an interesting story. He was an engineer who had worked on dams out west. Being a diver, he often did the inspection work on the dams. Going down with the other divers, he would check on erosion and silt buildup around the flood gates. Then he was injured on the job and won a sizeable compensation. He bought his camper, and he, his wife and young son took off to see the country and dive all the waters that interested him. He'd started in Colorado, went through the South then up as far as Maine. Of all the places he had dived Shinnecock Inlet was his favorite, because of the fish.

We dived together again several times before the end of the summer. I found myself envying the man. He was free, and he was spending his time doing what he wanted. But even before his compensation settlement, he'd managed to combine his favorite activity, diving, with his job, dam construction. I began to wonder if there was some way I could do that. I didn't want to get into another job that I'd just walk out on in a few months, but I didn't want to work in a gas station for the rest of my life either. I realized that diving had become the most important thing in my life. That was where I wanted to find my niche. But I had no illusions that anyone was going to hire me simply because I was a good diver.

I decided to go back to school to prepare myself for a real career. I would become a commercial diver.

CHAPTER 6

THE EDUCATION OF
A COMMERCIAL DIVER

The gap between sport diving and commercial diving is greater than most scuba divers realize. For instance, an 18-year-old called up our school not long ago to find out how to go about making his fortune as a commercial diver. Since I do all the commercial counselling at the school, which offers no commercial instruction, he was referred to me. He'd read an ad for commercial diver training, and said to himself, "Why not?" He knew he was a good scuba diver and saw no reason he shouldn't be as good a hard-hat diver.

Since he sounded so determined to try it, I suggested he come in for a chat. When he did, I sat him down and gave him some facts of life about commercial diving. I told him that it's not as simple or as glamorous as the ads make it sound because the ads are selling education, not diving jobs. I explained to him that diving isn't really the major part of the job. As Al Mikalow, who founded and runs the commercial diving school I attended, once put it, "Commercial divers are workers who dive, not divers who work. It's not just putting the suit on and going down. You have to work in the water, cold, miserable, under adverse conditions all the time. That's what you get your money for—hard labor underwater."

The boy nodded at what I had to say but he still wanted to try it. So I told him that he should find himself a job or attend a night school that would teach him welding and cutting. After two years of experience learning those skills, he'd be better qualified for the field and ready to enter a commercial diving school. He took my advice and is now enrolled in a night course in welding.

I don't try to disillusion divers about commercial possibilities, but I do try to give it to them straight. Matt, a cab driver who's about 40, came into the shop in April 1974 looking for advice about the commercial diving field. After taking into account my warnings about the difficulties, he entered a commercial diving school. Last spring I got a letter from him. He was working off the coast of Egypt on a drill ship, as a diver and making good money. It can be done, if you want it bad enough and you have the basic, God-given mechanical aptitude.

You can be taught about life support systems, the physics of diving, and valving systems for underwater oil pipelines. But nobody can teach you to be mechanically inclined. If you look at a nut and bolt and immediately pick up a screwdriver, forget about commercial diving. You may become the greatest sport diver in the world, but you won't make it as a commercial diver. Even being able to master one mechanical skill is not enough; you have to become a jack-of-all-trades —plumber, mechanic, welder, electrician and a few other things.

One reason I decided to try commercial diving was that I felt I had the necessary mechanical aptitude. And I had been sharpening it by working on cars at the gas station. I learned a lot at the school and later working on the Gulf of Mexico oil fields, and I value that experience now, even though it didn't last very long. For one thing, it has enabled me to do an occasional commercial job on the side, while I teach scuba to sports divers. For another, it gives me an option. When oil drilling begins in the North Atlantic off New York, I might get back into commercial diving. Most important, though, my commercial diving venture brought me into a very different and interesting world, one that few sport divers ever get to know.

The school that I selected from among the various ads was the Coastal School of Deep Sea Diving in Oakland, California. It was the biggest school of its type, had the most graduates in the field and, most important, at the time was the only school with instructors who were ex-commercial divers rather than ex-Navy divers. The Coastal School offered a 12-week course that seemed comprehensive.

I took off in September, though my classes didn't begin for two months. I wanted to take my time crossing the country by car: stop off to visit friends, camp, do some diving along the way. One place that I dived was Rice Lake in Ohio. I pulled into a deserted camping ground there early in October. I walked over to the edge of the dam and sat down, enjoying the warm Indian summer afternoon. The water looked blue and inviting, and I decided to dive the next morning. At 6:30 A.M. I was swimming underwater and came to the dam wall. I followed it up, and when I surfaced, ducks quacked and flapped all around me. Then I heard someone yell, "You stupid son-of-a-bitch, get outta there!" Duck hunters were behind blinds on the edge of the lake—angry, and with shotguns. I made a very quick apology before submerging, hoping I wouldn't be reminded of Vietnam.

The Coastal School didn't look like an ivy-covered Eastern college, but then I hadn't expected it to. It consisted of three ajoining airplane hangarlike buildings situated on an estuary of San Francisco Bay next to the 29th Street Bridge. I rented a furnished apartment across the bridge in Alameda.

My fellow students were a mixed lot, but many had worked on the sea. John Munley, from Virginia, was in the merchant marines, and Eric Dom was a mate on a supertanker who was picking up some schooling he needed for his master's papers. Three of the youngest students were from Alaska and had been working on salmon boats, making good money. This was their off-season and they had signed up for the school probably just as a lark, since all three took off back to Alaska before finishing the course. Another classmate, the son of a Los Angeles surgeon, C.L. "Jake" Jacobson, had studied cinematography at Southern Cal before deciding to become a deep-sea diver. We also had an Indian from Oklahoma who had been working as a court reporter in Hawaii; a convict taking the course through a California rehabilitation program; a middle-aged engineer who worked in the South Pacific. Roger Kerr, one I've stayed in touch with, was a roustabout in the oil fields of British Columbia.

Some of the students knew just what they wanted out of life; others hadn't the faintest idea. Mostly they were willing to give anything a try—they were gamblers.

They had to be. For commercial diving is a very small field with many dangers to it. Estimates vary widely, but most put the figure for full-time commercial divers at no more than 5000 as a worldwide total. One survey came up with 1800 full-time divers in the United States, with another 900 working part-time. Others put the figures even lower. The dropout rate is huge in the industry. Andre Galerne, a Frenchman who runs International Underwater Contractors, believes that you have to train about a hundred potential divers to get five full-time professionals working steadily in the field. One reason so many qualified divers quit for other fields is the difficulty of finding steady employment in commercial diving.

A majority of divers in the United States work in the Gulf of Mexico region, mostly on offshore oil rigs, and mostly for a few major diving companies. Others work freelance and part-time. Pay is not as much as some of the students who enrolled with me had hoped. For a harbor diver, one not working offshore, the median salary wasn't much better than $10,000 a few years ago. Freelance work seems attractive since divers contract for $100 to $200 a day, with extra pay for every foot they descend below 50 feet. But the work is so seasonal that most freelancers can't work steadily enough to total up impressive earnings over a full year. However, good divers working for a large company can make $30,000 a year —sometimes even up to $50,000—if they work on oil fields abroad.

During the first two weeks of the course we didn't go near the water. The first thing in the morning we had physical training classes, calisthenics and running more than a mile. It wasn't bad compared to the Marine Corps, but I wasn't happy having any reminder of boot camp. Diving is a physical activity, though, so we had to get in shape.

During the day we attended classes. At night they kept us occupied with heavy reading assignments plus two research papers. Two nights a week I spent at nearby Laney College, taking a welding course. My evenings and weekends were mostly spent in the library.

The academic work I enjoyed the most was the history of diving. Undoubtedly, people have been free diving since before recorded history; someone must have discovered he liked the taste of oysters and could dive for them, before anyone invented writing. But devices for underwater breathing also go back a surprisingly long way. In the fourth century B.C., Aristotle wrote about an inverted kettle, open at the bottom, which was lowered down to sponge divers; the divers could take a gulp of the trapped air and remain on the bottom longer. Alexander the Great is said to have used a diving bell in the Bosporous. If he did, it probably worked on the same inverted dome principle.

Some versions of the snorkle tube were probably used in ancient times, but for nearly two thousand years, no real advances were made to enable man to breathe underwater. Many inventors tried their hands but with little success. Leonardo da Vinci designed an underwater breathing device, but his invention was impractical for the same reason most of the others were: Man just does not have the lung power to suck air more than a foot or so underwater.

About 1615, Franz Kessler, a German, built a one-man diving bell. It looked like an inverted barrel, open at the bottom and shorter than the diver so his legs would extend below it for walking. The bell had glass view ports for the diver and had a weight that could be released for surfacing. It was still the old inverted dome principle. Edmund Halley, of the comet fame, came up with the first practical means to replenish the air supply, and he demonstrated it himself in the Thames in 1716. He went down 60 feet in an inverted dome, and new supplies of air were lowered in weighted casks from the surface. Divers could venture out from Halley's bell by means of hard hats with air hoses leading back to the bell.

By the beginning of the 19th Century, pumps had been developed that were able to send air down to divers below water. In 1837 Augustus Siebe, adopting the changes L. Norcross had made on Siebe's original design, perfected the immediate ancestor of present-day hard-hat diving dress. Siebe's outfit included a brass helmet with several viewing ports, a canvas dry suit, and a controllable exhaust that allowed the diver to change his buoyancy by letting more or less air into his watertight suit. This is the basic design used today.

Jules Verne wrote about the forerunners of self-contained underwater breathing apparatus in *Twenty Thousand Leagues Under the Sea* in 1870. The "Rouquayrol" apparatus he described, probably thought by most readers to be a product of Verne's imagination, was actually in use at that time. In this early scuba, air was pumped from the surface into a tank on the diver's back, and the diver could then detach the surface hose and breathe from a self-contained supply—but only for minutes. Even after scuba was perfected by Jacques Cousteau and Emile Gagnon in 1943, commercial diving was little affected. Scuba is impractical for 95 percent of a commercial diver's work. A diver doing hard labor underwater prefers his air supply not to be limited. Also, being connected to the surface in "tethered gear" allows for communication, which is of great importance in commercial work.

In the late 1950s, as oil companies began more offshore drilling, they started becoming dissatisfied with the performance of commercial divers. For a simple welding job that would cost only a few hundred dollars above water, an oil company had to shell out tens of thousands of dollars for divers to do the job.

Time was part of the problem. A diver working even briefly on the deeper jobs had to decompress for a long time. Eighty percent of our air is nitrogen, which under pressure dissolves in a diver's bloodstream. The pressure has to be eased off gradually or the nitrogen will form bubbles and the diver will have a case of the bends, which can incapacitate and even kill him. When mixed gases are used instead of air, the same basic decompression situation still applies.

Some oil companies experimented with robot diving devices, hoping to engineer the inefficient human diver out of the business. This was the stimulus the American diving industry needed. Between 1960 and 1965, diving became much more sophisticated in its technology. Larger companies began to replace the numerous tiny diving companies and one-man contractors. Diver training became more thorough. And by the late sixties, saturation diving, a major breakthrough, began coming into its own.

A diver can only absorb so much nitrogen (or, for deeper work, helium) into his system. Once he reaches the saturation point, additional time underwater doesn't require additional decompression time. Saturation techniques are now used for long and complex jobs at depth. Instead of having relays of divers going down, decompressing and coming up, the divers operate out of a saturation unit. They go to pressure only once and then stay there. For meals and rest breaks, the diver enters a dry, underwater, pressurized chamber. Overnight, the saturation unit, still pressurized with the divers inside, is usually hoisted to the ship's deck. Even if the job takes more than one day, the divers aren't decompressed until the job is over, and decompression is done in the unit on the deck while the ship sails to port.

All the large diving companies now have saturation units, with depth capacities of 600 to 1000 feet. Experimental dives have been carried out at 1000 feet, but few actual working dives have been done at that depth. Most units are now used for work in 300 to 500 feet.

The response of the diving industry to the oil companies' needs has resulted in enormous growth. While still a relatively small industry, the market for commercial diving services totaled more than $120 million in 1974, better than double the figure for 1971. Being tied to oil exploration obviously hasn't hurt.

After two weeks of class work, we began alternating our time between the classroom and the training tanks. In the last four weeks of the course we spent most of the day around training tanks or working in the estuary.

The main tank we practiced in measured about 30 feet across and 20 feet deep. Our class was broken up into seven seven-man teams, each designated by a color, and each assigned to a station around the tank. I was assistant captain of the orange team. One member of each team would be in the tank working on a project: welding, cutting, assembling or taking something apart. Some assignments we did standing on the bottom, others crouching, others hanging just below the surface. The water in the tank was always ink black, kept that way by dye. We could barely see the flame of a welding torch eight inches from our faces. We had to do all our projects by feel. This was important to our training since many commercial diving jobs are in near-zero visibility, especially in harbor areas.

Our team did well in these projects, as did the black team to our left. We usually finished ahead of the other teams, which left us time for fun. Once Eric Dom of the black team and I were in the water at the same time. I had 45 minutes to cut off three recessed bolts in a steel plate with a hammer and chisel. I finished well before my time and went over to check on Eric. He'd finished his project early too, so we leaned our brass helmets together for a conversation. Voice vibrations carried through the metal of those helmets almost as if they were sounding boards, but the constant hiss of air prevented Eric and I from conversing with ease, so I suggested to him that we turn our air off. We had about seven minutes of air in the helmets after shutting off the hose. I knew it wouldn't take the tenders above long to notice that no bubbles were coming up. My tender began to tug on my line. I didn't answer him, just went on with our chat. Finally Gary Conley, our British instructor, plugged in the phones and yelled down to us, "Alright, you bloody bastards, you've got two tenders up here scared to death. What've you got to say for yourselves?"

"We're just working away down here," Eric replied. "We can't help it if we don't need much air."

Eric and I used to plan to be in the water at the same time. Sometimes when we finished early we played football, charging into each other in slow motion. Because the black and orange teams spent so much time fooling around together, the others began calling us the Halloween team.

Learning the equipment is more important to a diver than any other part of his education. We started with the Mark

V unit, which is the classic brass helmet with viewing ports on the top, side and front and a rubberized canvas dry suit. It's a very bulky outfit, now almost outmoded, but it was a good one to learn on. We wore weighted diving shoes with lead soles weighing about 30 pounds a pair. We also had to wear a belt with 80 pounds of weight. This was in addition to a 54-pound helmet and 28-pound breast plate. The air in the suit makes the diver so buoyant that it takes all that weight to compensate. We had to learn to control the flow of air into the suit and therefore our buoyancy. Just to bend over, we had to adjust the volume of the suit.

One of the problems with the Mark V unit is its tendency to "blow up." This happens when the diver loses balance and allows himself to get into a feet-up position. Air then rushes into his legs, ballooning them and pulling the diver to the surface, feet first, at an accelerating rate as the air keeps expanding with the lessening ambient pressure. The helmet exhaust valve can't at this point get rid of the air. The suit may rupture from the expanding air, causing the diver to drown. If the suit doesn't rupture, the rapid ascent can cause the diver to wind up with a bad "hit" of the bends.

We were told that controlling the air in the suit while we were working had to become second nature. The easiest way to learn about equipment, for me at least, is to play around with it. After finishing a project, I would sometimes lie on the bottom in order to do a controlled blowup; we weren't deep enough for this to present any real dangers. I'd inflate the suit very slowly; then I'd raise my legs, letting them balloon. When my feet were floating above me, I'd crack open the air valve as far as it could go and shoot up out of the water feet first. Before the people at poolside could recover from their shock and identify who it was, I'd hit the dump button, a chin button that lets out the air. Then I'd blub-blub back to the bottom.

We had much more to learn about equipment than controlled blowups. The school owned most of the latest types of underwater gear, and we had to become familiar with as much of it as possible in the 12 weeks of the course.

The closest thing to scuba that we used was the hookah rig, often employed in shallow water dives. The hookah rig has a scuba-type regulator instead of an air-filled helmet. The regulator hose goes through a control system on the diver's back and then to the surface where they pump the air.

Between 80 and 90 percent of all commercial diving is done with compressed air. But the remaining 10 to 20 percent, which uses a mixture of helium and oxygen for depths greater than 150 feet, accounts for a disproportionately high share of the income. Oil companies are demanding greater depth capacities from diving companies because of the increasing depths they are reaching in ocean floor drilling.

As depth increases, compressed air presents problems to a diver. He begins to suffer from nitrogen narcosis—a completely separate problem from the bends. At normal pressures nitrogen is simply an inert gas, having no effect on the body. But under great pressure it can cause such strange physiological and psychological effects such as mental confusion, anxiety and lack of coordination. The point at which different divers become affected varies widely: It could be 80 feet, 150 feet or even deeper; and it may even vary for one diver from day to day.

We learned the effects of nitrogen narcosis when we went through the chamber familiarization exercises. The instructors put us in the decompression chamber and ran it down to various simulated depths. One day I would find myself unable to understand what was being said to me at a simulated depth of 150 feet; the next day I'd feel no change in my concentration down to 212 feet.

After learning about the chambers, we put on Kirby-Morgan band masks and entered the tank, breathing a helium-oxygen mixture. The first thing that hit me about breathing this mixture was how cold I felt. Helium seemed to draw the warmth right out of my body, chilling me to the bone. In fact, helium conducts heat away from the diver's body seven times as rapidly as air does. Since water temperatures are always very cold at great depths, various methods are used to keep a diver warm. Most common are the diurine suits, wet suits that have warm water pumped from the surface down through tubing in the suit.

The helium mixture also affects the diver's voice. It was a strange experience to hear my own voice sounding as if I were doing Donald Duck imitations. Helium-oxygen is much thinner than ordinary surface air and alters sound waves. In order to make the diver intelligible to the surface, helium unscramblers have to be built into the phone system.

Few of us would become divers immediately after graduation; we'd have to work as tenders first, which meant taking care of topside matters while the diver was working below. We learned how to operate the decompression chamber and the "rack," the console that feeds the diver his compressed air or his mixture of helium and oxygen, depending on his depth.

Oil being the major source of income for commercial divers, we had a special tank equipped with a well-head, the unit that tops the well on the ocean floor. Working on helium and oxygen, we would go down to inspect the closeoff rams on either side of the blowout preventer, which can be used to seal off the well—taking them apart and putting them back in. We also worked on "christmas trees" which are valving systems used in oil lines.

More fun than working in the tanks was working out in the estuary. On a sunken wreck there behind the school, we would practice salvage techniques. We'd make surveys of it one day, then do a salvage operation the next, trying out various kinds of diving gear. As a salvage project, our team decided to raise one of the two huge diesel tanks, which our instructors had told us were too rusted to bring up. We spent hours in the water working on it, putting patches on the rusted holes and pumping air into it. I was in the water with John Munley, and we overstayed our time getting the tank ready. Finally the succeeding team of divers convinced us to come up and give them a chance, and John and I went out for lunch.

On our way back, we were approaching the estuary when we heard a whoosh and saw the tank rising from the water like a Polaris missle. While we had been out to lunch, the next crew in the water had gotten hold of a much bigger air compressor and that had done the job. The tank began floating out toward the shipping lanes and a Coast Guard boat came by, instructing us by bullhorn to get that tank out of the channel, which we finally did.

We all were laughing and enjoying our success, but since John and I hadn't been in the water when the tank came up, we decided to bring up the second one as well. By this time, we had already fulfilled our underwater requirements for graduation and we had to talk Gary Conley into letting us work on the tank.

The second tank was a tougher job. Since it was filled with silt, we had to jack the tank out of the water with a one-ton "come-along." I worked the compressor hose from below and John sat on top of it, cranking away on the come-along attached to the bottom of the work-barge ladder. The tank started to lift, so I backed off. Then the come-along snapped and the tank fell, rolling over. For a frightening minute or so, I thought John must be pinned under the tank, and he thought I must be, our diver-to-diver communications having been knocked out. The water was totally murky as I moved through it, feeling with my hands for John. Finally we found each other, safe and sound. The brief experience reminded us, though, that we were indeed in a risky business.

We spent the rest of the day breaking two more come-alongs, then hiding them in the tool shed so the director wouldn't find them. We never did get that damn tank up.

Graduation came soon after that. We celebrated with a heavy drinking party at the British Pub in Oakland. It was February, and the diving season didn't really get underway along the Gulf Coast until May. I decided to head back for New York, work at the gas station and then drive to Louisiana, with enough money saved to hang on for a while.

CHAPTER 7

BAYOU BLUES

In the black hours of a March morning, I drove the 75 miles from New Orleans southwest to Morgan City, along winding bayous—a few isolated shacks the only signs of life, the radio my only company. About 4:30, as I approached a bridge, I could see the mist reflecting the glow of a city. The top of the bridge gave me a view of an alive waterfront. Men hurried about between the lights and the shadows, working on barges, moving cargo containers, operating cranes. Welding torches flashed from shipyards.

This was Amelia, a bustling little town, and another bridge led across Black Bayou into Morgan City itself. Morgan City is not an Easterner's idea of a bayou town in the Mississippi Delta. Though its population is under 17,000, it doesn't look small because it's highly industrialized. The 38 major diving companies in the Gulf area, which account for 80 percent of the commercial diving business in the United States, are concentrated in and around Morgan City. Some salvage diving is done, but the source for almost all of a diving company's work is the oil industry, with its 6000 or so drilling rigs and production platforms extending from the bayous more than a hundred miles out into the Gulf.

The road leading into town was lined with shopping centers, bars and fast food joints, many of them open. Not trusting my stomach to Cajun cooking at this hour of the morning, I chose a Burger King, then found a motel.

I arrived on a Monday morning and gave myself a week to find an apartment and get settled before starting my job search. On Thursday I rented a furnished bungalow in Patterson, just outside Morgan City. The landlord, J.C. Camp, worked in topside construction on the oil rigs. He'd recently bought the property and built two bungalows for rental, while he and his wife lived in a mobile home.

Early Monday morning I started my search for a job. Coastal School had given us a list of all the companies in the area. Students who had sent out letters and resumés while we were still in California had gotten back noncommittal letters, suggesting they come by for an interview when they were in the area. Seeing these responses, I didn't bother writing before I came. I knew a diving company would want to see my body, standing and sweating in their doorway, before they'd consider hiring me, a diver with little previous experience.

The first place that I applied was Oceaneering International, one of the giants of the field, with offices in Houston, Santa Barbara and British Columbia as well as in Morgan City. Three hundred of the company's 400 full-time employees are divers, and many other divers are hired freelance during the peak season. With an annual volume of $10 million, Oceaneering is as dominant a force in commercial diving as General Motors is in auto manufacturing. The company also does its own research, operating a hyperbaric medicine research center in Houston which has pioneered exotic gas mixtures for deep diving.

New divers like myself are generally hired as tenders, at a salary then of $7000 a year. After 9 to 18 months of on-the-job training, the tender might become a diver, making about $12,000. The larger corporations—Oceaneering, Ocean Systems Inc. and Taylor Diving & Salvage—have moved away from the practice of contracting with freelance divers in favor of building up their own full-time staffs. They'd rather train their own divers and have them around whenever they need them.

My dream was to work freelance, so I fantasized that Oceaneering would have just landed a big new contract and would be signing up all the freelance divers they could get hold of when I walked in the door. That happens occasionally at the height of the diving season, when companies get into a bind and hire any qualified diver they can find. Realistically, though, my best bet was to be hired as a tender. I was confident that I could work my way into the diving job I wanted before long.

I liked the look of Oceaneering. Inside a handsome brick building was a carpeted reception area with paintings decorating the walls. After I told the receptionist I wanted to apply for a job, the personnel man came out, gave me an application form to fill out; then he called me into his office. We discussed Coastal School and my background. I had listed a number of freelance jobs I had done in New York, mostly fixing bent props on private boats. He told me that nothing was happening in diving at the moment, but later on, when the season picked up, they might start hiring again. He suggested that I drop in every morning to see if anything had come up.

I walked out feeling reasonably pleased. It was all so cool and professional, I felt as if I were back in New York. And I hadn't expected to get a job right away. I then called on the other companies on the list.

Ocean Systems, Incorporated was another comparative giant, with 125 full-time divers, though it didn't give quite the smooth corporate appearance that Oceaneering International did. Formerly part of Union Carbide and now a subsidiary of Samson Cordage, OSI was responsible for some of commercial diving's major technological breakthroughs in the 1960s. They developed a very sophisticated ADS (advanced diving system) for saturation diving. With this system, divers compress in a DDC (deck decompression chamber), then transfer to a PTC (personnel transfer chamber) and ride that to the work site. At its hyperbaric research laboratories in Tarrytown, New York, OCI has been experimenting with neon as a substitute for helium in deep diving.

When I walked into the Ocean Systems offices, several people were just sitting around. They told me OCI wasn't hiring then because nothing was going on at the moment. I could see that for myself, since the phones weren't even ringing.

I had a hard time locating the next place on my list, though I drove back and forth in front of it several times. I had been expecting something more than the small storefront I finally found. I quickly came to realize that an enormous gap, in style as well as size, separated the major diving companies from the smaller outfits.

That first day set my routine for the next several weeks. I'd get up early and begin a regular round of calls on companies: Oceaneering International, Ocean Systems and a few others. The man at Oceaneering encouraged me to keep coming back. The others only gave me a quick, "We don't have anything, sorry." But I figured that my persistence might impress them if something did come up.

After eleven every day, I had nothing but free time. I'd go to the library and read up on the area, or to Riviera beach and do some scuba diving. I bought myself an inflatable rubber boat and did some catfishing on the bayous. On weekends, I'd sometimes drive up to New Orleans. I was relaxed, just biding my time, because I knew the diving season didn't really get underway until May.

In the evenings, I learned about the commercial diver's world by hanging around the divers' bars. Gary Conley, my instructor at Coastal School, had told me where to go: Lil's Elbow, the Checkmate Lounge and the Nightlatch. Divers, coming back from a job, would often have a wad of money to blow and weren't reluctant to spend it in bars. Miniskirted waitresses would encourage the flow of green bills.

At Lil's Elbow one night I ran into a schoolmate from Coastal. He too had found things to be slow. The only ones from school who had gotten jobs so far were a few who'd come down right after graduation. They'd filled the few job openings and now things would have to wait until the season picked up.

Lil's Elbow had more than its usual share of divers hanging around, waiting for the diving jobs to start coming. Many were itinerant divers, just arriving in town in advance of the diving season. These were the veteran freelancers who didn't want any part of a salaried job. They liked to make the big money whenever and wherever they could, then pick up other kinds of work when the diving business was slow.

The freelance divers are very mobile, independent men. Most have wives and families and places they call home. But when a good paying job comes up, wherever it is, off they go, sometimes for a few days and sometimes for months at a time.

The seasonal nature of the business left room for these freelancers. While diving companies preferred to keep their divers on payroll, they couldn't afford to carry all the divers they might need during the peak season. So they kept a file of freelance divers they could call when they needed extra help.

These men had to be good divers to survive this way. They relied on their reputations to get work regularly. Freelancers earned $100 to $200 a day base rate; depth pay, below 50 feet, ran a dollar a foot, of which the diving company took 40 cents and the diver 60 cents. They were often called old-timers, but that was a relative term. Most were in their thirties, not many over forty. They had come in with the diving boom in the sixties and managed to stick, many others having drifted off or dropped out. It's hard to find a diver who has been in the business for two decades. Before 1950, for instance, there were only 800 full-time professionals in the world.

Typical of this breed of freelance diver was a man I knew only by his nickname, Pappy Yokum. I'm not sure why he was called that. He certainly didn't look like the old character by that name in Li'l Abner, though in other ways he might have been a character out of that comic strip. He was tall and lanky, with black curly hair and the kind of weathered face that you often see on men who've worked outdoors in strenuous labor all their lives. His age seemed indeterminate, but must have been in the late thirties.

Like many divers I met down there, Pappy had a very questioning mind. He was interested in many things. We'd trade books and get into discussions about everything from religion to science. A friend of my landlord, J.C. Camp, with whom he shared an interest in ham radios, Pappy had been diving in Louisiana for a long time, though he was originally from Mississippi (most of the people I met in Morgan City were from other states originally). Pappy was always telling me that a smart diver makes as much money as he can as fast as he can, then gets out, using some of his earnings to set himself up in business. He considered it foolish to think of continuing to be a commercial diver all your life. The risks of getting injured or killed were just too great. Pappy was saving his money to buy a mobile-home park back in Mississippi. He was able to sock away a fair amount because he earned a lot. Pappy had a fine reputation as a diver and was kept on call by many of the major diving companies. Off-season, he applied his mechanical skills to a variety of non-diving jobs.

Pappy liked the freelance style of diving, not just for the money but also for the freedom. He could say, "I just don't feel like working today," and not work. He could also decide not to make a particular dive that didn't feel right to him without answering to anyone but a temporary boss.

"A good diver has to watch out for himself," Pappy would tell me, and not leave his safety up to anyone else, whether it be his tender on topside or his buddy on a sport dive. A diver's time in the water means money to a company so they try to get the maximum time out of a diver. But when Pappy felt he'd had enough for the day, no person or company could force him to dive again. Pappy would speak with wonder about divers who didn't have this attitude about watching out for themselves—especially the Cajun divers who often paid no attention to decompression limits. They could dive anytime they could make a buck at it.

Cajuns were the only ones I knew from the delta area who worked as commercial divers. Most Cajuns came from poorer backgrounds than the other divers, with less education and opportunity to make a good living in other fields. The money in commercial diving looked even better to them than to most of the rest of us. So they took more risks.

I remember standing at the bar one night in Lil's Elbow. I noticed a fellow at the end of the bar who looked to be in bad shape. When he reached for a drink, his arm didn't seem to function right. And when he got up to leave, his walk was somewhere between a limp and a shuffle. I asked who he was. "Oh, he works in a diving company office," I was told. "Used to be a good diver, but he got bent too many times."

Getting the bends is, of course, a diver's occupational disease. It can kill you when you get a "hit." But, coming up from a dive, a hit might be so minor a diver doesn't even notice it—just a slight pain in the elbow or the knee. Eventually these nitrogen bubbles kill too many of the diver's tissues. His movements become stiff, because the joints are most vulnerable to hits. In divers' bars, I often saw men who looked and moved as if they had just been beaten up in a fight—stiff, favoring a leg, not using one arm much. A diver can wind up a cripple if he's not careful.

Many mathematical tables have been worked out to determine decompression rates. Individual diving companies often work out their own; they want to get the absolutely maximum safe "optimal working time" for a diver in the water. So many variables are involved in getting the bends, though, that a diver can never feel totally safe just following the company's schedule, since for the company time is money. The amount of underwater working time a company wants from a diver may be too close to the margin of safety. The way a diver feels that day or the extra exertion of the underwater job he has just done may push him over that margin.

The problem comes up most often in repetitive diving. A pipeline is leaking oil and the diving company figures that two teams of divers, each diver in a team making two 50-minute dives, should be able to find and repair the leak. Each diver takes his turn, then each diver "repets," goes down again. The second go-around still leaves work to be done, and the first diver is asked to repet again. As far as the tables go, it's theoretically possible. But if the diver doesn't feel right about it, feels that he has pushed his body hard enough already, he might say, "Look, I've had enough for today." The diver has to know his own limitations and refuse to go beyond them. He may get himself into trouble with a boss for refusing to dive, but the other divers won't criticize him.

Some divers go even further, becoming downright superstitious about when they should or shouldn't dive. The day is bright, the weather calm and warm, and everything on the oil rig seems to be in order, but when his turn comes, the diver decides this just isn't his day to dive. Perhaps some sixth sense tells him to say no. A diver has to have a very solid reputation to get away with that; if a newcomer tried it, he'd be looking for another job very shortly. Some diving companies will accept these occasional refusals from an otherwise capable diver, knowing that it wouldn't make sense to insist he perform a job when he's psychologically unfit to do so.

A diver faces other dangers besides the bends. As the technology of diving gets more complicated, more mishaps can occur with the machines or their human operators. Not long before I arrived in Louisiana, a team of divers had been killed. Over beers at Lil's, I heard several different versions of exactly why and how it happened. Most of the divers I talked with, however, told this story: Two divers in a saturation unit had finished their work below and were hoisted to the surface. The divers would begin their decompression when their unit was mated to a deck unit. The divers probably thought they were in good shape; they were out of the water now, and all they had to do was decompression time. Then, apparently, a tender made a mistake in reading the gauges. The pressurization between the two units had not been equalized, but thinking it had been, the tender opened the hatch between them. The two divers were sucked into the hatchway and crushed to death.

It was May; the weather was hot; and I was learning about the diving business in bars instead of in the water. I had figured on spending some time looking for a job, but now I was beginning to get frustrated. The diving season should have been getting into full swing but it wasn't. Record spring floods along the Mississippi had disrupted normal waterfront and marine businesses, causing a delay in the diving season.

I was also beginning to get bored and lonely. There wasn't a hell of a lot for a city boy to do down in bayou country. Women my age were either married or had gone to the big cities, and I had little in common with the single women who had stayed behind.

In late May, Marie, the girl I had been dating in New York, wrote to suggest that she come down for Memorial

Day weekend. I agreed eagerly. We had a great time together those three days; we went to the beach, did some catfishing in the bayous, and talked about what was going on in New York.

When she left, loneliness hit me hard. I'd been in Morgan City three months. Seeing Marie made me realize how much I missed New York and my friends back there—to say nothing of just missing being with a woman.

I not only felt out of place in the bayou country, I looked and sounded like an alien. It seemed I was the only male down there wearing long hair except for the teenagers. Those in my age group, mid-twenties and up, looked like Elvis Presley, but I wasn't about to start combing my hair into a DA just to fit into their lifestyle.

I found the people friendly, but I had a hard time relating. I'd be having a friendly chat with a local in a bar when suddenly, for no reason I could understand, he would take something I'd said amiss and say, "You lookin' to get your jaw broke?" I made a deliberate effort to stay out of barroom trouble. I was afraid that if I did get into a fight, the whole populace would rise up and take the opportunity to railroad the New Yorker out of town. Besides, they carried guns, and not just in the gunracks of their pickup trucks.

I was in a bar one night, talking with a group of people, when a woman in the group asked me to dance. She was blond, older than I was and had a teased hairdo. I said sure, and we got out on the floor and danced to the juke box music. When we returned to the group, everyone continued taking with everyone else, and a little later, she and I danced again. When I got back to the bar this time, a man in the group asked me what I was drinking. I told him my brand of Scotch and he ordered it from the bartender.

"You know why I bought you that drink?" he asked.

"Well, to be friendly, I guess."

"No. I bought that drink to tell you, in a nice way, if you

dance with my wife once more, I'm gonna blow a hole in you."

With that he pulled open his jacket to show me the gun stuck in his belt. While I was trying to figure out how to respond, the bartender leaned over and said, "I heard that, and I'm not having any of that stuff in my bar." He reached under the bar and slapped a revolver down on it. "And if there is any shooting, I'll do it."

After that things quieted down. I explained to the man that I didn't know it was his wife. He said, "Yeah, I know that. It wasn't your fault." Which left me wondering why he threatened to shoot me if he didn't hold me to blame. I didn't dance with his wife again.

Anyway, country and western music isn't the best kind to dance by, as far as I was concerned. And country and western music was just about the only music played in those bars. When I would walk into the Checkmate Lounge or Lil's, I'd be carrying a pocketful of change to play the few rock songs they had listed. You'd know I was in there if you heard "Layla" by Derek and the Dominoes playing as you came in the door. Then my money would run out and Johnny Cash or some other country and western singer would come on, and everyone else in the place would brighten up.

By this time I was thinking of packing it all in and heading back to New York. What stopped me from leaving was my next door neighbor. A few weeks after I moved in, the bungalow next to mine was occupied by a diver named Don Brumfield, and it was Don who eventually got me my work as a diver.

A thin six-footer with dark hair in his early to mid-thirties, Don came from Arizona. He'd been diving freelance in Louisiana two years before. Then in the off-season he'd gone back to Arizona to work in construction, doing occasional freelance diving on the side, and he stayed for two years. Recently, he'd decided that the best money was in Gulf diving, so back he came, to work another season.

Don, an experienced diver, had earned himself a good reputation among the diving companies. But it took him three weeks to land his first freelance job. Some companies had offered to hire him as an employee, but he had refused. He saw no reason to take a $12,000 salary for diving when he could make more than that back home in Arizona in construction. He had returned to Louisiana to make good money, at freelance rates, not to find security.

Don complained about the work situation that season. He also remarked on how the entire personnel he knew from two years ago had changed, except in the front offices. After three weeks, though, he finally hooked up on a freelance basis with a diving company in Amelia: S&H Diving. I had never gone there on my job search.

I used to drop by Don's bungalow to watch television with him in the evenings and talk about diving. After Marie's visit, we became closer. He had a wife back in Arizona and was missing her. Now I knew how he felt.

Two weeks after Marie left, I went to New York for a friend's wedding. I left early Friday and got back on Monday morning. As soon as I walked in my bungalow, Don came over and asked, "Where the hell were you on Friday?"

"New York, for a wedding. Why?"

"Because, I might have had a job lined up for you, that's why."

On Friday he'd gotten a job on a rig for the weekend. He knew that the company was short-handed and could have used a second diver. He would have recommended me but he didn't know where I was.

I cursed myself, my luck and my New York friend for getting married at the wrong time. But Don assured me that the diving season was finally getting into full swing and that there'd be other opportunities.

It didn't take long. On Wednesday, my phone rang and it was Don: "Jimmy, get your ass down here. I think I've got these guys talked into believing you're a diver."

I got my ass down there.

CHAPTER 8

WORKING ON THE BOTTOM OF THE GULF

I knew when I came down to the Delta that I couldn't expect to work as a diver right off the bat. I thought I would be hired as a tender by some company, then work my way into a job as a diver. Then eventually I'd go freelance and start making the big money.

Now Don had cut the process short by several steps. My first job was to be as a freelance diver. I had no idea what Don had told the people at the diving company. I knew he couldn't have told them that I was a beginner who'd never even been on an oil rig as a tender. I had butterflies in my stomach as I drove over to the company in Amelia to meet Don. I was afraid that someone would ask me all kinds of questions about my oil field experience, then laugh at me and throw me out. Well, the only thing to do at this point was to fake it.

I walked into the office, trying to look like a salty old hard-hat diver, and asked for Don. I was told he was out back. Good, I thought, maybe he's alone and I won't have to meet anyone. I found him loading hose into his Chevy pickup truck. And standing next to him, chatting away, was a portly man I knew had to be with the company.

Don saw me and said, "Marty, this is Jimmy, the guy who'll be diving with me."

"Jimmy, Don tells me you haven't been a diver for long,

but he says he's worked with you and you know how to handle yourself."

"Sure, right."

Marty had a skeptical look on his face, but he shook hands and wished us luck. As soon as we got in the truck, I asked Don what was going on. He told me that the job called for two divers. The company didn't have another one available at the moment and was about to search around their free-lance listings to find another when Don volunteered, "Don't look any further. I've got just the guy for you." Since the company didn't know me, Don said he'd subcontract me for the job. So technically I was working for Don rather than the company.

We stopped at the Nightlatch for a beer and skull session. I confessed to being a little nervous about the job and told Don I was worried that I might foul him up. "Hell, Jimmy," he said. "You want to be a diver, the least I can do for a friend is get your foot in the door. Now it's up to you. You screw up, it won't hurt me any. Besides, this is an easy dive. Nothing you can't handle."

He went on to explain the job. We'd have to leave about two the next morning and drive down to Cameron, Louisiana, to board the crew boat going out to the rig. The boat would take four or five hours to get there. A diving crew had just finished laying a pipeline off the rig, and our job was an inspection dive, to see that the work had been done right. Don would tell me what to do and what to look for, step by step. We wouldn't be doing heavy labor or working deep, so we'd use our own wet suits and Don's Kirby-Morgan band mask, the air-breathing device most commonly used on shallow dives. Since only one of us would be in the water at a time, we could share the mask. Two tenders were already out there; they'd been with the other diving crew.

We shot some pool at the bar, then went back to Don's place and he whipped us up a packaged food dinner. We talked until eight when I decided I'd better try to get some sleep. I didn't sleep very well. Had I overreached myself again? What if I couldn't handle the job? What the hell, I told myself. What can they do to me? If they say, "Sorry, pal, you blew it," well I blew it. At least I'll have had the chance.

At 2:00 we got into Don's pickup and drove to Cameron. We wandered around in the humid darkness, up and down the docks looking for the boat. Crew boats of all sizes and shapes docked there, from 60 feet to 160 feet. They serviced rigs all over the Gulf. Get aboard the wrong one, and you might wind up a hundred miles from where you're supposed to be.

When we finally found the right boat and climbed aboard, Don picked himself a comfortable spot on the back deck next to our bags, said goodnight and fell asleep. I was too wound up to sleep. I watched the crew loading the boat with boxes of supplies for the rig. As I sat alone in the dark, the creaking and easy rocking of the boat relaxed me, and I dozed off.

I woke up somewhere in the Gulf with the sun near the horizon and no land in sight. I could see clusters of oil rigs in every direction. The rig we eventually approached was a "mother" rig to a cluster of satellite rigs surrounding it for about half a mile. Pipelines ran from each of the satellites into a junction box which joined them to the main pipeline running from the mother rig to the shore.

The huge flat platform was held above the water by three rows of steel beams, descending into the water, four legs in each row. The platform had only one level, unlike many of the other rigs, but it seemed massive, the size of several football fields. The whole thing seemed to be crammed with sheds, barrackslike buildings, cranes and tanks. Dominating the platform was the oil derrick in the center, as high as a 15 story building.

I could see as we approached that the rig was a submersible one. That meant those 12 huge legs of steel rested on pontoons that sat on the bottom of the Gulf. With the pontoons empty, it had been towed out to the drill site, a giant barge. Then the pontoons were flooded until they sank to the bottom.

Another type of rig is the semi-submersible, in which the pontoons, partly flooded, float below the surface and don't rest on the bottom. Anchors hold the structure in place. The jack-up rig, a third type, looks like an erector-set construction. It rests on three massive caissons, legs that can be moved up and down. Then there's the drill ship, simply a ship with a hole running through the center of it for drilling.

The captain of the crew boat took us within inches of the ladder and hovered the boat there while we climbed off. Then they tied her up to unload the supplies.

The deck level was a confusion of machinery and people. Cables and power lines ran everywhere. Roustabouts were moving large crates. A welder burned his torch into some tubing on the side. The busiest place was the "moon pool," the drill hole in the center of the platform with the oil well derrick over it. There the driller was shouting something to his crew of "roughnecks" who were hurrying about. Masses of machinery and equipment of various kinds were piled around. Later I sorted out where things were, what some of the machinery was and how to find the crews' quarters and the mess hall. But at first, it all seemed a jumble.

Don set off to find the "toolpusher," the foreman who is directly responsible for everything that happens on the rig. I followed Don's every footstep. I was on board as a diver and didn't want to make any blunders and give anyone a clue that I wasn't the veteran diver I pretended to be. Besides, I could easily have gotten lost.

Nobody paid much attention to us, though. Everybody had his job to do and kept busy at it; they lived on the rig, but we divers were only transients, passing through from time to time.

Don found the toolpusher at the moon pool, and he briefed us on the details of our assignment. The previous diving crew had worked from a barge, laying pipeline and connecting the sections together. They'd run risers, the vertical pipeline sections that clamp to the rig's legs. The diving company had another job lined up, so they had left the inspection work to be done by a later crew. We had to make sure that the risers were clamped to the legs securely. Then we'd move along the pipeline, 160 feet down, checking it for leaks or damage and seeing that the clamps and flanges were properly aligned and seated. The pipeline had been filled with air so we could detect leaks by the air bubbles it would give off. We also had to inspect the weight coating, eight inches of concrete poured into a collar around the pipeline to protect it and hold it down, to see that it hadn't cracked or broken off.

The toolpusher talked fast, and I kept my mouth shut during the briefing, just nodding at everything he said, knowing I could ask Don later about the parts I didn't understand. We then walked over to the diving station, while Don told me how to go about checking these things. The diving station wasn't ideal. All kinds of pipes ran through the area, but then an oil rig isn't set up for divers. The station had two decompression chambers. Air lines ran from the decompression chambers to the air compressor then to the operator's rack. In case anything went wrong with the compressor, the tender had pressurized air in the decompression chamber to pump down to the diver.

The tenders helped Don and me suit up. Attached to Don's mask was an umbilical cord composed of three separate lines strapped together every ten inches: a communications line, air hose and kluge. The kluge is a small diameter hose into which air is pumped from topside to determine, by a gauge that calibrates air pressure, the diver's depth. The tender has to know this depth at all times in order to calculate decompression times and in order to calculate the diver's depth pay. The umbilical sometimes includes a lifeline, but if the communications cord is strong enough, this isn't needed.

We were both scheduled for 50 minutes bottom time, the usual work schedule for a diver in these particular conditions. After 50 minutes, a diver is too cold and tired to be efficient. Given this depth and time, we would have to make decompression stops on the way up, then have a spell in the decompression chamber.

A tender checked Don out before he entered. Then Don jumped into the water, while the tender "fished" him—fed him the right amount of line while making sure it didn't snag on anything. A good tender can keep just enough tension on the line so he can not only feel where the diver is at every moment but can even tell what the diver is doing. Divers who like to think of themselves as being in a glamorous business consider tenders their squires and sometimes expect them to perform the duties of a butler or manservant. Some tenders are happy to do such personal service, looking toward the day when they too will be divers, fully knighted with a tender squiring to their needs.

With Don down below, I said nothing to the tenders. I didn't want them to find out that this was my first time on an oil rig. They might be apprentice divers who felt they deserved a chance for advancement and were being bypassed. And my lifeline would literally be in their hands. While the two tenders talked, I stayed with the communications equipment. I kept my ears glued to the phones to hear every word Don was saying, because when I went down, I wanted to sound exactly like I knew what I was doing.

After 50 minutes on the bottom, the tenders began bringing Don up. After he made his water stops, hanging off for a while in progressively shallower depths as part of his decompression, they brought him to the surface. He then had five minutes to get out of his wet suit and into the decompression chamber. A diver never wears his suit into the chamber, because if he has any oil on it, he's bringing a combustible element into a closed area that has oxygen equipment in it. If a fire ever starts inside a chamber, there's not much that can be done for a diver in there.

Don briefed me quickly, telling me where he'd left off in checking the risers and pipeline and where I had to start. I put on the Kirby-Morgan band mask and adjusted it. I looped the hose underneath my left arm and clipped it to my diving harness. I had made my own diving harness, with brass rivet reinforcements, and thought it looked pretty sharp. I took the bailout bottle and hooked it in back of the harness. Instead of running the bailout bottle's hose into my mask, I attached it to a regulator and clipped the regulator to the right side of my harness, as Don had done. The bailout bottle is only used in emergencies, when the air supply is cut off. Though it can be hooked up to the mask, most divers use a separate regulator. No sense in having emergency gear depend on a mask the diver might have to ditch in an emergency.

Getting ready for the dive and checking the equipment had relieved my jitters. I coiled a couple of wraps of the umbilical in my left hand before jumping in order not to pull the tender into the water. Then I jumped. I headed down the rig's leg, and hadn't descended more than 15 or 20 feet when I was distracted from my thoughts about the job. Out of the depths hundreds of sleek, mean-looking fish charged up, looking as though they were going to tear me to pieces. Barracuda! I'd never met a school this large before and I was scared. I'd been told that they weren't really dangerous, despite their nasty reputation, but they sure looked dangerous, flashing their sharp teeth at me. I shut my eyes and stayed still for a moment. Nothing happened—I didn't feel my arm being bit off. I opened my eyes again and saw the barracuda hovering all around me, top, bottom, left and right. Just hanging there, looking, their big jaws working, but staying about six feet off. I started moving down again. The barracuda below me parted while the ones above closed up behind me. Obviously they weren't anxious to kill me. I was glad of that.

Barracuda are often attracted to divers because the bright flash of metal triggers their feeding instinct, reminding them of the small silver fish they eat. After hanging around awhile, they finally caught on that I wasn't some tasty little fish, and they went away.

I moved down the riser, checking the clamps. In my tool bag I had a hand wrench which I used to see if the bolts could be loosened. If they could, I wouldn't try to tighten them with a hand wrench—it's hard to pull on a wrench underwater. Instead, I would have told the tool pusher who might have then assigned us to tighten the bolts, if he happened to have hydraulic tools available. If not, a later crew would do the job. I looked for the bubbles that would have indicated a leak, but found none.

At 90 feet down, the water was clear. Around a rig there's some surface pollution, garbage that falls or is thrown off the rig. Oil rigs have helped pollute the Gulf of Mexico. In the old days they dumped their garbage directly into the Gulf. Now, however, under pressure from environmentalists, they're much more careful about everything from oil leakage to garbage disposal.

Oil rigs alter the marine environment in positive as well as negative ways. They provide marine life with artificial reefs. Barnacles attach themselves. The fish that feed off barnacles gather. Other fish make their homes around the legs, seeking protection from their natural predators, which, in turn, are attracted to the rigs. Many rigs have become homes for jewfish, a large grouper weighing 600 to 700 pounds. A couple of years ago a giant jewfish swallowed a diver whole, and, like Johah, the diver survived to tell the tale. His umbilical wasn't severed, and a fellow diver had to kill the fish to rescue him.

I saw one 80-pound grouper, a curious and friendly fish which didn't try to swallow me. The bottom I was moving along was flat and sandy, not mucky as I had expected. "All bolts are tight on flange number two," I told topside. As I moved along the pipeline, I found places where the weight coating was cracked, but nothing that looked serious. I was pleased with that, since I wasn't anxious to offer the tool-pusher my opinion as to whether major repairs should be undertaken on the pipeline.

It didn't seem that I had been down for very long when the tender said, "Get your tools together and get ready to come up." They always warn a diver five minutes ahead of time in case he's in the middle of a job. I started back along the pipeline and got myself in position. "Ready to come up," I said, and they hauled on my umbilical until I was about 60 feet below the surface. There I made the first water stop on my decompression schedule. I held onto a steel bar on the rig's leg for the 15 minutes or so.

The tender figured out the stops and times based on the company's decompression tables, watching my kluge to make sure I didn't ascend faster than the prescribed rate. "Okay, coming up again," he told me, and I was brought up a little further for another stop. It felt strange, just hanging there. At first I thought of myself as a yoyo on the end of a string. Then it struck me: I was a worm on a hook. I wondered if any sharks were in the area.

While hanging there, the tender asked me if I wanted anything in the decompression chamber. I asked him to get my sweatsuit and a book I was reading out of my gear bag, and also a cup of coffee. When I was brought to the surface, the tender helped me out of my wet suit. I was in the decompression chamber well under the five-minute time limit. The chamber measured about ten feet long and had oxygen masks hanging on the side. When the pressure of the chamber was brought close to surface pressure, the tender asked me to breathe some oxygen from time to time. That speeds up the decompression by allowing you to breathe off more nitrogen, normal air being 80-percent nitrogen. You can't breathe oxygen at much depth, though, since it can be toxic under pressure. Every 10 or 15 minutes they changed the air in the chamber, flushing out the old and pumping in new without changing the pressure. The loud hiss would have kept me awake if I'd been tempted to fall asleep. I drank my coffee and read my book, feeling very good about things. It was late afternoon by the time I got out of the chamber.

Don and I went to the mess hall to get some food. We were served all the fresh shrimp and rice we could eat. Food hadn't tasted so good in months, and it wasn't just my appetite. Workers on the oil rigs eat well. Usually, two selections are served, corresponding to the two dominant groups of workers on rigs: Southern whites have a taste for ham and greens cooked in fat, and Cajuns prefer spicy shrimp dishes. All workers have to be fed well; they put in 12-hour days of hard labor for 14 days at a stretch. Then they have two weeks on shore to rest or, as many do, pick up some extra money moonlighting.

After dinner, I walked around the rig, looking the place over. It was still buzzing with activity. Drilling goes on 24 hours a day. Roustabouts, the manual laborers, were hauling 100-pound bags of chemical mud. They pump that down the drill hole to lubricate the drill. It has a very sour smell, especially when combined with men's sweat, but I got used to it after a while.

Movies were being shown in a recreation room, but I was too tired for that. Most of the workers who were off duty must have been sleeping. The few I saw who weren't working were playing cards.

I sat near the edge of the rig and smoked cigarettes while

watching the sun go down. Some rigs have strict rules forbidding smoking, but this one didn't seem to. The breeze was cool, a welcome relief from the muggy Delta evenings. Even more welcome was the absence of mosquitoes; we were too far out for them here. I felt at peace, and bone tired. I wasn't worn out from physical labor; that hadn't been too hard. It was the emotional release of having gotten myself through a trial I'd been anticipating for a long time.

We finished the inspection dive on the second day, then the third day the toolpusher asked us to check for erosion around the base of the rig; undercurrents swirl around the rig's legs, tending to undermine it. He also said to search on the bottom for tools. When they have divers handy with nothing else to do, toolpushers often assign them this job. Many valuable tools drop overboard.

I found a couple of crescent wrenches, ratchets and chucks. Old pipe was lying on the bottom too, but they weren't interested in that. While Don was down a welder dropped something overboard, right where Don's bubbles were coming up. I worried for a minute, but Don never even saw it. That's one reason many divers like to wear helmets, even though they're more clumsy than the masks.

On the fourth day, there was no more work for us to do, so we sunbathed until the crew boat came to take us and the tenders back.

That was the beginning of a regular work schedule for me. The diving company was busy now, and they kept moving their divers from rig to rig for various jobs. For the follow-up inspections, they hired Don. Two divers weren't always needed, but when they were, the company accepted me as Don's partner.

The jobs began to feel routine to me. The sense of adventure faded quickly and diving became a job, often a tedious one. An oil rig is not a place where you'd want to spend a vacation. The life out there is a hard one for everyone.

Divers have less actual working time on a rig than the other workers. When I had time to kill after a dive, there wasn't much to do to amuse myself. Off-duty workers either slept or played cards. Often, I hung around the moon pool, watching the driller and the roughnecks do their jobs. The driller is captain of the drilling end of the operation, a highly respected figure not only on oil rigs but throughout the Coastal region. They made about $18,000 then, a top rate in the industry. The driller's crew, the roughnecks, are the best paid laborers on the rig. This is hardly surprising, when you consider that a company can make or lose thousands in minutes, depending on how quick and efficient the driller and roughnecks are.

On one rig I heard someone complaining to the driller that the bit was "walking left." The driller decided to pull it up. This sent the roughnecks into action. They disassembled the drilling shaft into 30-foot sections, weighing 300 pounds each, as it was hauled up. Then they stacked them into racks. When the bit was replaced, the process reversed. A roughneck, on a day when the bits have to be changed, can lift several tons in his 12-hour shift.

While the bit was being changed, I asked the driller, who seemed unoccupied for the moment, what was going on. He told me that he was replacing a three-toothed bit with a two-toothed one that he didn't use much because it had a tendency to "walk right." The compensation worked. When the drilling resumed, someone yelled, "It's back on track."

I asked the driller how he knew what was going on way down on the ocean floor. "Well, when you've been working these rigs as many years as I have," he told me in a Mississippi drawl, "you get to know a few things." We got to chatting, and when he found out I was from New York, he said, "I figure I might be working up there myself before long. I hear there's going to be some offshore drilling around Long Island pretty soon."

After my dive the next day, while I was decompressing, I felt low and all the frustrations of my situation in Louisiana began churning through my mind. At the Coastal School, I had learned about meditation from Gary Conley, who pointed out that it can be very helpful when you're spending long hours in a decompression chamber with nothing else to do. I concentrated on one scene to relax my mind: the view from a mesa in Colorado National Monument, where I'd seen a whole valley unfolded before me, a desert shimmering with many colors.

My mind and body relaxed after a while. Then I began to think about my situation. Was this really what I wanted? First, I knew I didn't like living in the Delta. I was lonely. I missed New York, my friends back there and my lifestyle.

Second, I was disappointed in the kind of diving I was doing. I had not gone into this business with rosy-colored visions of being paid to enjoy myself underwater. But it's one thing to know that and it's another to experience it. It was tough, often boring work, and dangerous. I'd seen enough ex-divers by now to know how the bends can cripple you.

Third, the economics of my situation were not good enough to justify it. I was now making good money freelancing, but that depended entirely on Don's connection with the diving company and the fact that the season was at its peak. Once the season was over, Don planned to head back to Arizona. He saw that freelance possibilities were drying up, and he probably wouldn't come back the following year. My only chance to hang on in Louisiana once he left would be to go to work on a tender's salary. And I could make better money than that back in New York.

But it was what the driller told me that tipped the scales. The whole field might be booming in New York before long. I wouldn't have to abandon entirely a commercial diving career if I left now. If I wanted to try it again when drilling started off Long Island, one of the major drawbacks would have been eliminated—living in Louisiana.

On the way back to Patterson, Don and I stopped in a bar, and I told him of my decision to move on. He'd been expecting it. I felt a little bad telling him, since he'd gotten me into the business. But he was heading back home himself, and he understood and agreed with my decision.

The next day I packed up and drove north.

CHAPTER 9

PASSING IT ON

When I got home from Louisiana, the first thing I did was head for Cougar Sports, my second home.

John Schuch started Cougar in 1958 as a combination pro dive and archery shop. In 1959 he added the Skin Diving School of New York. The only national scuba training organization at that time was the YMCA. In 1961, when the National Association of Underwater Instructors was formed, John was at their first East Coast clinic. For the next few years, the instructors at the school were either NAUI or YMCA trained. Then John joined with other pro dive shop owners in 1967 to form the National Association of Skin Diving Schools, and they began their own instructors' training program. For some years now, the school has been one of the largest on the East Coast.

I chatted with John about my experiences in the Gulf. He told me that the shop got quite a few calls asking for various commercial diving jobs, and he suggested that I handle these. I readily agreed. It meant that I could continue making some of my living, at least, as a diver. Then as I was about to leave the shop, Bruce Carnase, who was then director of the school, yelled, "Hey, Jimmy, don't go yet. I've got something I want to talk over with you." We went back into his office, and he asked me if I'd like to join the school's staff of instructors. Scuba diving was booming, and the school had more students signing up for courses than the present staff could handle.

I'd never given any thought to teaching scuba diving, but as soon as he said it, the idea sounded good. He explained that I'd work as an assistant to an instructor for a time. Then, when he thought I was ready, he would send me to one of the NASDS clinics, where for a week I'd be tested as an instructor. If I passed, then I'd begin teaching at the Skin Diving School of New York.

Bruce had a class going at the time and assigned me to assist him. Bruce was a fine scuba diver who had been a teacher in the New York City school system. Teaching scuba, he'd tell me, was like teaching any subject: It's not just how much you know but how well you're able to convey your knowledge. And in scuba, you have to deal with students' natural fears and build up their confidence in order to make them into competent divers.

I saw how Bruce kept excellent control over his class. The students felt confidence in him because he was sure of himself. He turned part of his second class over to me and liked the way I handled it. By the end of the course he decided to send me to the next instructors' clinic, which was to be held in Newport, Rhode Island, at the end of the summer.

Meanwhile, I was assigned to assist Charlie Greutzner, an instructor who later became one of my good friends. "You're going for your tests in a couple of weeks," Charlie said to me, "so you might as well begin teaching now, with this class. I'll be sitting back and watching, letting you know if you screw up." After the first class, Charlie critiqued me. "You did fine, except you kept sticking your pinkie into your ear every few minutes."

"But I had water in my ear."

"That doesn't matter. The thing is you've got to make your students concentrate on what you want them to concentrate on, and that's not your ear. You were distracting them."

After every class Charlie reviewed with me what had happened. By the time the course was over, I'd had a good crash education in teaching scuba.

Five of the 12 assistant instructors on the staff, those Bruce felt were now qualified to become instructors, were sent to the Newport clinic: Pete and Les DiMichael, two brothers; Mike Arnoff, an easy going nice-looking chap; Don Arrington, a detective on the New York City homicide squad, who would be teaching the school's underwater photography course; and myself. Bruce would be at Newport as a member of the national staff that was doing our testing.

When we arrived on Sunday our motel was filled with NASDS people, about 100 of them from all over—California to the Virgin Islands, Oklahoma to Canada. From Sunday through Tuesday we had a busy schedule of tests, plus classroom work to prepare us for teaching. Tuesday evening we had oral testing, which meant giving a five-minute talk before a class. I thought of myself as a good talker, but I'd done no formal public speaking before. I felt apprehensive before my turn came, thinking this would be the test in which I might do poorly. But then, standing before the class, it all seemed so natural and easy that I relaxed. And I received a top grade.

On Wednesday and Thursday, we had water tests, a welcome break from the classroom. I felt confident, knowing I could perform well in that element. Besides, I knew the diving area like the back of my fin; Don Arrington and I had been diving in Newport regularly for a long time.

On Friday ratings were handed out to the candidates. Four ratings were given: Instructor Provisional means that you can teach a basic class under the supervision of someone with a higher rating; as Instructor, you can teach the basic class; an Open Water Instructor Provisional can teach the advanced class, under supervision; and Open Water Instructor is the top rating, enabling you to teach any class. All five of us from the Skin Diving School of New York received OWI, the top rating. Bruce was in his glory. We'd see him approaching others on the national staff with the news, saying, "Yep, that's the way we train 'em at our school."

The five of us were not only pleased for ourselves and our school, but also, in a slightly chauvinistic way, for the East Coast. All scuba divers know that scuba activity centers in Southern California. About one out of four American divers lives there, where they have the weather to dive all year around. And Florida divers also have the advantage over us, in weather and water conditions. Sometimes we East Coasters can get a little defensive about it.

That night the NASDS staff hosted a banquet for all the new instructors, with wives and girl friends in attendance. Our group sat together, except for Pete DiMichael, whom no one could find. John Gaffney, the executive director of NASDS, was on the podium making a congratulatory speech, when someone walked in the door dressed in full scuba gear. Our table began howling, for we immediately recognized Pete behind the mask and wet suit. He flopped his way to the podium in his fins, shouldered John out of the way and said, "I'm pleased to announce that the following have been admitted into the East Coast Full Foot Fin Fun and Fan Club." Pete had spent the whole afternoon drawing up very artistic scrolls, which he now presented to each national staffer, together with some good-natured abuse. "I now want to call up the Gaff, the man who has done the least to make this week possible. . . ." Pete berated him some more, handed him his scroll, kissed him on the forehead, then shoved him back into his seat.

That loosened things up quite a bit, and we all had a high time that night, especially us East Coast divers. Toward the end of the banquet, Bruce came over to ask if I was heading back that night. When I told him yes, he said, "That's good, because then you have a class in the morning."

My first class, which had eight students, was typical in many ways. It was held in Nyack, New York, up the river from the Bronx, at a small pool our school had rented for the class. Our school gives classes all over the metropolitan area, renting pools from the YMCA or schools.

Our school doesn't have a formal swimming-test requirement before enrollment, though we do ask each student to rate himself as a swimmer. Most rate themselves conservatively. If anyone gives himself a low rating, I sit down with him and find out if he is capable of taking a scuba course. In addition, the first thing I have a class do is swim several lengths of the pool, so I can see for myself how well each of them handles himself in the water.

The best swimmer in this first class of mine was Jan. I found out later that she had been on a swimming team in high school, which didn't surprise me. Now she attended the University of Miami, studying oceanography, so she had a professional reason for wanting to learn scuba. But it wasn't just her swimming ability that made me believe from the first that she'd become an excellent diver. It was the way she seemed relaxed in the water, as if she were in an environment natural to her. Even good swimmers don't always have that manner.

After the first class, the student I expected to have the most difficulty with the course was John. He had a slight build and, though quite adaquate as a swimmer, he seemed to be both nervous and awkward when he had to do an exercise, such as free diving. I knew that his trouble stemmed from lack of confidence. I guessed he had always been nonathletic and had done poorly competing in sports. Now he felt he was in another sports competition and expected to fail.

Scuba does require making a physical exertion, pushing

your body to some degree and using muscles that most people rarely exercise. But our association has tried to get away from the idea of scuba diving as a competitive sport. With the equipment that's available today, anyone in decent health who knows how to swim can have access to the underwater world. That's the way I teach it.

I took John aside and told him, first, that I was convinced he was capable of becoming a scuba diver, and, second, that he was not competing with the rest of the class. It didn't matter at all if the others learned an exercise faster than he did. He could go at his own pace and that would be sufficient for learning. "Take it easy, John, you don't have to rush it," I said. "If you don't get it the first time, just try again. And if you're still having a problem, we'll work on it during the free period." I leave time at the end of a class so each student can practice on his own, with my assistant and I there to help anyone who needs it.

Once John, a nice guy who tried very hard, became convinced that he could go at his own pace, that he wasn't in an athletic competition he was going to lose, he relaxed. By the end of the course, he was as competent a scuba diver as anyone in the class, except for Jan.

Unlike John, Hal was an athlete. He taught karate at the local YMCA. But he also had a confidence problem. He'd become frustrated and angry when he couldn't master an exercise immediately. Then he'd begin gagging on the water. I'd watch him struggle, then tell him, "Hal, the water isn't an opponent. You don't have to chop at it. Relax a little. You're not out to defeat the water, you're out to cope with it." One day he stood up in the middle of the shallow end of the pool, pulled off his mask, looked around and said, "What am I doing here? What the hell am I doing here?"

I didn't believe Hal should quit the class, because I felt sure he could handle it. I encouraged him and kidded him on. And once he concentrated on an exercise, he mastered it in no time. Finally he caught on and passed the course with no problems. After the open-water test, he took me aside and said, "You know, Jimmy, you're a really good teacher." I thanked him, but then he went on. "No, I mean you're even better than you think you are, for a reason you don't understand. You see, you taught me scuba diving, and I am—or was—totally afraid of water."

I saw Hal not long ago. He came by the shop and told me he and his wife had been diving down in the Caribbean a few times. They aren't scuba fanatics by any means, but they do go a couple of times a year and enjoy it. The idea of scuba had always appealed to Hal so much that he'd finally decided to try to overcome his fear of water by taking my course. Besides, Hal had exaggerated this fear of his. Real hydrophobia is something I can do nothing about, no matter how well I teach.

Confidence is the key to learning scuba diving. But before the student can have confidence in himself, he must have confidence in his instructor. I run a relaxed class: I joke with the students, tell them stories about my experiences, and we have fun together. To me, it's much easier to win students' trust this way than by acting the role of the Marine Corps drill instructor. They're not taking the class in order to be terrorized, they're there to learn an activity that is supposed to be fun. So I make the class fun, but I always let them know who's in charge. I don't allow students to compete with me for the attention of the class. If one does, I tell him, "Look, this is *my* class. I'm the only one allowed to show off here."

I tell entertaining stories about my experiences, but stories that also make the point that I know about scuba. At the same time that I'm building the students' trust in me as an okay guy, I'm building their trust in me as a competent diving instructor.

To transfer the students' trust in me into confidence in

themselves, the most important thing is being patient with them. Before I started teaching, I would have guessed this would be difficult for me. When I go diving for my own pleasure, I become irritated if my buddy holds me back because his diving ability or experience doesn't match mine. But I haven't found this to be true in teaching. I never expect too much of students who are just starting out.

I know that they're going to make mistakes and will look and feel awkward at the beginning. They'll flop around like seals on land. But my natural impatience is overcome by my pleasure in watching them learn. The first time we use regulators in the pool, I have the students lie down in the shallow end and just breathe. I lie down with them, and they don't know it, but I'm getting almost as much a charge out of the experience as they are. I see their eyes glow with excitement and pleasure: "I'm underwater and I'm breathing!" their expressions say. I feel elated that others are finding out how great it feels, and I'm the one who turned them on to it.

Impatient teachers often make the mistake of doing things for their students rather than making the students do for themselves. For instance, if a student takes a mouthful of water, gags and tries desperately to get out of trouble by swimming to the edge of the pool, I don't grab him and pull him out. He has to learn to handle these situations himself. I swim to within a couple of feet and coax, "What's the first thing you do when you're in trouble?" If all I've told him about throwing off his weight belt doesn't snap into his mind, even after I repeat the question, then of course I'll pull him out. Most of the time, once he knows I'm not going to take care of things for him, he'll remember to throw that weight belt. And he'll gain the confidence that next time he finds himself in trouble, he'll be better able to handle it.

A student diver has to learn from the beginning to do for himself, even in minor ways. I remember one class I had with a girl who was always complaining, "Oh, Jimmy, I can't carry that tank. It's too heavy."

"I don't want to hear it," I'd tell her. "Get that tank on your back and walk to the end of the pool."

I wouldn't let the girl con any man in the class into carrying her tank for her. A tank is heavy, but a diver, man or woman, sometimes has to carry it. I expect the same things from my woman students as from my men. In that way, I'm for women's lib. And I've found that women appreciate it. They don't want to be babied.

Occasionally, I have gotten students that I couldn't teach. All teachers do, I'm sure. And though I know it's inevitable in a certain percentage of cases, I always feel a sense of failure. We have six pool sessions, preceded by a poolside lecture. The seventh session is a written test, together with some general discussion. Then the eighth is the open-water test. By session four, I usually have made my decision about what to do with the problem student.

If it doesn't look at that point as if he can catch up with the other students, even with some special attention from me or my assistant, I sit him down for a discussion. I suggest that he start from the beginning with another class at the school. I tell him that he's too far behind now, and it's not fair to him because now he'll just keep falling further behind. And with a new class he'll have a headstart, and perhaps he'll learn better from another instructor.

I won't let a student continue in my course if I don't think he will qualify as a basic scuba diver by the eighth class. If I have any doubts about a student's ability to pass the open-water test, but don't think he needs to be recycled back to the beginning of a course, I might have him take a couple of brush-up classes before letting him take the test. We don't run a diploma mill, and I don't want my name on an unqualified diver's certification card.

At the end of the course, each student fills out an unsigned evaluation of the course and his instructor and turns it into the school. Occasionally, some student will complain that the lecture material is too heavy. But that's the problem with a course geared to a wide range of intellectual abilities and educational experience. We do a fairly complete coverage of everything in scuba diving, from the laws of physics to the mechanics of the equipment. But I feel it is necessary to give the student enough theoretical background so that he understands this alien environment he's entering, how it affects him, and what he must do to cope with it. He must also have confidence in the equipment he uses, and this comes from knowing about it.

We don't try to make the written test we give in session seven too severe, but we do have students who fail it. One who failed was a journalist who had been an honors student in college and graduate school. He went in overconfident, and had to show up on another day to take the makeup test.

My classes have included quite a variety of students: lawyers, doctors, secretaries, truck drivers, construction workers, factory workers, bartenders, college students. I've found among them many different reasons for deciding to become scuba divers. Some get into it because their friends or family dive. Others have tried snorkling on a Caribbean vacation and liked it, and now want to take the next step. Jacques Cousteau's television programs have turned many on to diving. If anything unites all these people, it's their eagerness to try something out of the ordinary.

Because they have paid their money to learn and are anxious to become scuba divers, they are usually good students. They listen, follow instructions and are excited about each new step they take. There are, though, exceptions to that rule.

Some are victims of the "Manhattan syndrome." Non-New Yorkers might call it a New York syndrome, but being from the Bronx, I believe it centers in Manhattan. What I mean is a distrustful attitude, an expectation of being ripped off. While waiting for me to reveal myself as a secret agent for the most expensive regulator on the market, the student doesn't even hear what I say.

Take Fred, for example, a psychiatrist in his late twenties who shared an apartment in Greenwich Village with two girl friends, who were also enrolled in the class, one in which I assisted Bruce before getting my instructor certification. Perhaps Fred's sessions with his patients got him into the habit of not listening, for nothing Fred was told seemed to lodge between his ears. Except when he was told about equipment. Then he'd listen carefully, just to avoid following the instructions. For the second class he was told all students were required to have a 15-pound weight belt, and Bruce made some suggestions about the right kind to buy.

I didn't notice Fred's belt until halfway through the second class. The students were practicing free diving, and when Fred did his, he came up gagging, tore the snorkle out of his mouth and called for help. I swam over and said, "What's the first thing you do when you're in trouble, Fred?"

"I'm drowning!"

"Fred, throw your weight belt."

"Help me!"

He wasn't going to do it himself, so I dove down and grabbed for the breakaway release buckle. There was none. I grabbed at the belt, pulled and pushed and finally the thing came off, and I popped back to the surface with it. With his weight belt off, Fred had enough buoyancy so that he was floating with his head well out of the water, still spitting some water but getting his breath back. I looked at the weight belt I'd taken off him, trying to figure out what the hell it was. Then I realized: That was a Ford emblem; it was a car seatbelt, the kind where you have to push on the emblem for the thing to open. I couldn't believe it at first, but there it was —Fred's homemade weight belt.

I'd have to discuss that with him later, but first I asked him how he had just gotten into trouble.

"I can't understand it," he said. "I did my free dive alright, but when I got to the bottom, I couldn't breathe through my snorkle."

"You couldn't what?"

"I couldn't breathe through my snorkle."

"Wait here, I'll get Bruce, maybe he can help."

I swam to the other end of the pool and told Bruce, "Come with me. You've got to hear what Fred just told me." Bruce swam back and Fred repeated what he'd said. For a few seconds Bruce was dumbfounded. I could see him wondering if he could possibly have given the wrong impression about a snorkle's use, but no, everyone else was clear about it.

"You dummy!" Bruce finally yelled. "You don't breathe through a snorkle underwater, don't you listen?"

"I didn't hear you say that."

Fred learned nothing from that little experience. The next class, when the students were supposed to have underwater gloves, Fred showed up with a pair of Nanook-of-the-North style gloves—fur, inside and out, for underwater use! Finally, though, Fred did catch on, and by the last two classes, he must have decided to pay attention. He passed his open-water test, wearing a regulation weight belt and regulation gloves.

The largest category of difficult student is the scuba widow. These women enter our school solely because they're tired of staying at home while their husbands or boyfriends are out scuba diving. Vivian, a quiet, attractive brunette, was one.

She came to me after the second class and said, "Jimmy, I just can't do it. I want to quit." I asked her why she'd signed up for the class, and she explained that it was because her boyfriend was a diver. I knew that was the wrong motivation for trying scuba diving, but I asked if she really thought she'd like diving herself, not just to be near her boyfriend. She said that she thought she would. I told her that if she wanted to, I'd make a diver out of her. I'd spend a little extra time with her, but she had to give it an honest try. She agreed.

Vivian had to struggle through the next two sessions. I'd work with her during the free period, telling her she could do it, just try again, don't get discouraged. Then, in the fourth class, we had the doff-and-don exercise, in which the student takes off his tank underwater, and then puts it back on. This is the toughest exercise for most students, so I took Vivian aside and gave her some encouragement, then had her try it. When we came back to the surface, I said, "See, Vivian, you did it. You're going to make it as a diver, that proves it."

Until then Vivian had been the most reserved student in the class. Now she began yelling and screaming, "I did it! I did it! Goddamn, I did it!" After that, everything changed for her. Once she was convinced she could do it, she really began enjoying diving.

But it doesn't always work out that way. Take Brenda, for instance. She'd already been in two other instructors' classes and had been recycled back to mine for her third try. Her student history card, which had been passed along to me, stressed her seeming awkwardness in the water and her tendency to panic. I tried my best with Brenda, but nothing seemed to work. After the third session, I sat down with her to discuss it. She told me that her husband was a diver and had encouraged her to try it. She thought she'd enjoy it, if only because she could see her husband more often.

I probed a little more and asked if she had any idea why she was having so much trouble.

"Well," she said, "I didn't mention it to the other instructors, but I have this condition. I'm hydrophobic."

"Hydrophobic? Are you sure?"

"Yeah, my doctor told me that. I can't stand water in any form. I even hate it running on my head in the shower. But I thought maybe I could overcome it by taking scuba. Having an instructor tell me how to get along in the water would make it alright."

"Look, Brenda," I told her, "none of our instructors are psychiatrists, and none are God. I can't just go, 'Zap! you're no longer afraid of water.' And knowing this about you, I can't certify you as a diver, because someday in the water you'd panic and get yourself hurt. I don't think you should be taking scuba at all."

Brenda's face lit up with relief. She thanked me for my honesty and for trying to teach her. She didn't even want to discuss a refund. She'd just been waiting for someone with authority, a professional, to tell her she wasn't capable of scuba diving, so she wouldn't have to feel bad about quitting.

Next to the scuba widows, the worst students are those who take up scuba to prove something to themselves. I had one student, George, who had a problem. With breathing gear on, he refused to venture out of the shallow end of the pool. I tried to help him. I took him by the hand, keeping his facemask six inches from mine, and brought him slowly to the deep end. When we reached the deep end, I backed off two feet from him, then put my arms out to indicate, look where you are. He looked around, then shot for the shallow end and wouldn't come back. After class I spoke with him.

"George, just what's the problem? It doesn't make sense to learn scuba diving if you don't ever want to go into deep water."

"Look, I really appreciate that you're trying to help," George replied, "but I know my limitations. I thought I could make a breakthrough, but I can't. . . . What I mean is that I'm a coward."

"You're afraid of deep water?"

"No, I'm a coward. I'm afraid of everything, always have

been—subways, muggers, dogs, everything. I thought I could conquer it by learning to do something dangerous like scuba diving, but now I realize I can't."

"Well," I said, not quite knowing what to do with him, "we could recycle you. Maybe if you started fresh in another class. . . ."

"Oh no, it's no use. I'm sure of that now. But I would like to come to the rest of the classes, if you'll let me stay in the shallow end of the pool."

George attended the rest of the classes, staying in the shallow end, usually with one hand held against the wall. He'd breathe underwater and could even clear his mask and regulator underwater, but only in three feet. I never quite understood it all, but George seemed to be enjoying himself there. I didn't, of course, take him to session eight, the open-water checkout.

The day of the open-water test for the basic class begins at 7:30 on a weekend morning—not my favorite time of the day—when I roar up to Cougar in my van, putting on a show, yelling for coffee. That's the appointed time for my class, and usually a couple of other instructors' classes, to gather for a two-hour bus ride to the Quarry in Hamburg, New Jersey.

I fully expect every student of mine that's on the bus to pass the test. I won't let any student come to the open-water test if I have any doubts about his ability to handle it. The only trouble is, sometimes the students are not as sure of their abilities as I am.

Left to themselves, I know that some would start worrying about the test, working themselves into a state over it. So I focus their attention on me. I talk about my seedy adventures of the previous night, or my hopes for future nights.

"Hey, Diane, when are you going to break down and let me show you a good time?" I might call out.

"Like I told you, Jimmy, I've got a good man already."

"But how do you know I'm not better until you give me a shake?"

Pretty soon a whole busload of students is trying to figure out whether or not I'm serious about asking out Diane. Sometimes I'm trying to figure out the same thing. Usually only Diane knows whether to take me seriously or not.

I keep up the jovial, good-time feeling right up to the water's edge. Then the joking stops. The Quarry is a small, protected, but fairly deep lake on the site of an old rock quarry, a good place for novice scuba divers. First, the students do their free diving. Then they return to shore and don their scuba gear and come back out. One by one, I call the students over to me, telling them exactly what I expect them to do. Then I get each student to lock eyes with me and we descend, face to face, not more than two feet apart. If I see the student's eyes grow extremely wide, I know he or she is getting apprehensive, so I reach out and hold his or her wrist. That touch gives the student enough reassurance to fight down any rising panic.

The test itself requires them to do no more than they've already done in the pool, so if I can keep them calm and in control of themselves, they find it easy. We rise back to the top and the student yells, "Hey, I made it!"

"Of course you did, Diane, now about that date. . . ."

Later we all go over to the Quarry restaurant to have beers and celebrate. I want this first dive to be a good time for each student, a good experience above and below the water, so he'll try it again.

I tell the students about the school's advanced diving course and about the trips and dives that the shop runs. I do most of my diving with groups from the school and shop, and I like to see my own students get into these things and begin diving with us. I like to have smiling faces around me when I dive—and well trained divers.

I encourage the students to call me anytime they have

questions about diving, or just to drop in the shop to say hello. Once I've taught a student scuba diving, I feel that a personal connection has been established between us that I like to keep alive.

I was sitting in a restaurant with Fran, my date, John, a friend of mine, and his date Karen, a striking woman with long blond hair. Fran said to me during dinner, "The people at that table near the wall are staring at us."

"Yeah, it's Karen they're staring at," John said, and Karen just smiled.

"Can't you guys see it's me they're staring at. *I'm* the star attraction at this table," I said, also knowing that it was Karen.

As we got up to leave, someone shouted from the table, "Hey, Jimmy, is that you? Come over here!" It was Vivian. I turned to John and said, "I told you so," and went over. Vivian introduced me to her boyfriend, now her fiancé, telling him I was that "super scuba teacher" who taught her how to dive when she was ready to give up on herself. I was pleased to hear the good words, but even more pleased just to see Vivian. I felt I had an important relationship with her: I had turned her on to diving, something I enjoy so much and something she now enjoys too.

And that is why I like to teach scuba diving.

CHAPTER 10

BAD DAY AT NEWPORT

In the summer of 1974, the Charter Boat Owners' Association of Southern California issued a protest letter to all scuba instruction associations. The letter complained about a decline in the standards of that year's crop of newly certified divers, which, it said, had led to increasing numbers of accidents. This protest was one item in a chain of events that led to a law controlling scuba diving in Los Angeles County, a law the entire scuba world united in opposing and which has since been repealed.

Not having dived there in a couple of years, I don't know the situation in Southern California. It may well be that the charter boat owners had a valid complaint. But I wonder about something else: What were they doing taking out newly certified scuba divers for open-water dives in the Pacific on their boats?

The C-card that a diver receives after successfully completing a basic course should not be a passport to any scuba adventure he chooses. He has only established himself as qualified to begin scuba diving, not to enter every phase of it.

More and more, the national scuba certifying organizations are stressing the importance of advanced courses. PADI (Professional Association of Diving Instructors) plans to eventually discontinue the basic course as a separate entity and combine it with their advanced course. At our shop, we charter boats for wreck diving and night diving, and a diver has to have an *advanced* certification card to come along on these trips.

When a diver receives his basic certification card, I tell him about the diving that's available to him. There's no sense in him spending his money on a basic scuba course and then having no place to dive or no one to dive with. So our shop runs many diving activities open to basic divers, ranging from treasure hunts at the Quarry in northern New Jersey to trips to the Caribbean.

I urge my new divers to participate in as many of these group activities as possible. They should get the feel of diving in some safe body of water like the Quarry, which has no tides or currents to deal with. After doing almost all of their learning in a pool, new divers are not ready to plunge into the North Atlantic and explore a wreck.

I stress the rule of never diving alone and urge that they try to dive with someone they can learn from, some-one a little more advanced in diving. After that, if they decide they want to get further into diving, they should sign up for the open-water course, the advanced scuba training our school offers. To become proficient in his sport, a diver has to learn many things beyond what can be taught in a basic course. He can learn them on his own, but if he's too foolhardy, in too much of a hurry or doesn't have the right diving partners, he can easily get himself into trouble. He's better off learning open water diving from a professional instructor.

The water sessions for our open water course are held in Newport, Rhode Island, with the lecture sessions given back at Cougar. The course includes such areas as underwater navigation, coping with tides and currents, orienting yourself to the local diving environment, calculating air consumption and night diving. Then once the student has completed the other classes, we have optional classes in repetitive and deep-diving techniques and ice diving.

In one way the advanced diving is more fun for me—I'm teaching in open water rather than in a pool. But I'm not providing students with their first experiences of diving, and in that way it's not as much fun as the basic course. In the advanced classes students have quite a mixture of diving experience. Some have just completed their basic courses, others have been diving for years. These veteran divers sometimes have to be broken of bad habits they've picked up over the years. And they're usually not as easy to teach; often they come into the course with a know-it-all attitude, and I have to convince them every step of the way.

The open water also provides far more opportunities for students to get themselves into trouble. Take, for example, the worst day I ever had as an instructor.

I was teaching three classes that weekend at Newport. I had finished my Saturday morning class and had gathered my four afternoon students on King's Beach. I reviewed with them what we were to do: They'd follow me as, using snorkles, we swam out past the rocks near the beach to a buoy I'd set 100 yards offshore. Then they'd go down the line in buddy teams, clear their masks, attain neutral buoyancy and set off on a straight compass run.

I swam out, using the snorkle and kicking with my fins, moving at a slow, easy pace, looking back occasionally to see that they were following close behind me. When we all got to the buoy, I signalled, "OK?" and each of them signalled back, "OK!" I sent the first buddy team down the line, then followed halfway down, to keep my eye on them while waiting for the second team. But this time, only one man came down the line. I signalled, "Where's your buddy?" He looked around and shrugged. I motioned for him to join the other two at the bottom of the line, then headed back up to find out what had happened to Howard, his buddy.

I saw immediately that Howard was in what's called "surface emergency panic." His eyes were as big as teacups, he was huffing and puffing as if he'd just finished a three-minute mile, and he was clinging to the buoy for dear life. He had a control buoyancy jacket (CBJ) that would keep him well above water if he'd inflate it or if he'd throw his weight belt. Panic often makes a diver forget the easiest and safest thing to do. Howard was not an experienced diver, having earned his basic certification a short time before beginning the advanced course. In the first two classes, though, he didn't seem to have trouble keeping up with the others.

"Howard, throw your weight belt," I said to him, very calmly. "Relax, take it easy now, but throw your weight belt." Howard didn't hear anything I said. He was in such a shocked state, he just stared past me. "Damn," I thought to myself, "this is going to be one of those days."

I deflated my CBJ, to approach him from below the water and get his weight belt off. Below water is the only way to approach a man who thinks he's drowning. If you're on the surface he'll try to climb on you, but he won't duck below the water to grab you—that's the last place he wants to go.

As soon as I got his weight belt off, Howard came to life. With a lunge, he began swimming toward the beach. I couldn't head after him while I had three other divers below, waiting for me and not knowing what to do. I descended quickly, told them to come up, and when they did I said to inflate their jackets and swim slowly to shore. Then I headed after Howard.

As soon as I began to close in, I yelled, "Stay away from the white water!" The white water was caused by swells breaking over rocks, and rocks are a very dangerous place for any diver, much less a panicked one. Sure enough, Howard headed straight for the white water—because he saw a rock there he could climb up on. It was closer than the beach and he wanted to get out of the water as soon as he possibly could. He went through the white water and climbed up on the rock. Thank God, I thought, he made it without getting smashed by a wave.

The next step would be getting him off the rock. At least he was safe for the moment. I decided it'd be best to give him a minute or so to calm down, while I swam back and got his weight belt. I told him, "Relax, don't do anything, I'll be right back." It took me only a couple of minutes, and when I returned, I laid Howard's weight belt on the rock. The waves bounced me against the rock a couple of times. I wondered how Howard had managed to get up there. He must be lucky, I decided. I hoped his luck would hold.

Howard meanwhile just stared out to sea. I could tell that he was still freaked out. The tide was coming in. I'd have to talk him off that rock before some wave washed him off it. I yelled to catch his attention, and when he looked at me, I began giving him step by step directions for taking off his tank. "Reach for the belt with your left hand. Now pull the buckle . . . the other way. Okay now, Howard, listen, I want you to. . . ." Howard followed the directions, but he still wasn't himself. He acted like a zombie.

"Now, Howard, I want you to stand up, and walk to the back of the rock, where it's protected. When I say, 'Jump,' I want you to jump in and swim to shore. It's not far." I felt as if I were talking a man in off a ledge, except that I was trying to convince him to jump.

Howard had me worried. Usually a diver will quickly recover from panic once his head is safely above the water. But Howard still seemed to be in shock. However, he followed my directions, jumped in and swam to shore. I swam in after him, took off my tank and weight belt and left them on the beach. Then I swam back to the rock, put on Howard's weight belt, and was putting on his tank when I saw the biggest wave of the day about to crash down on me. I tucked the tank under my arm, stuck the regulator in my mouth and dove off the protected side of the rock, just as the wave pounded down, covering the whole rock. When I returned to the beach, I gave Howard his equipment and chatted with him. He was still dazed but beginning to sound coherent. Then I gathered the other three students, put on my tanks and went back out to complete the exercise.

Why did Howard panic? Probably because he started to hyperventilate. The association between uncontrolled hyperventilation and panic is close and operates in both directions. Panic causes anyone to breathe more rapidly, and when this happens to a diver, who has to be especially conscious of his breathing, it can lead to hyperventilation, which is overbreathing, gasping for more breath than the body needs. But the reverse can also be true: Hyperventilation may come first and cause a diver to panic. (Controlled hyperventilation, in which a diver deliberately overbreathes to purge the carbon dioxide from his system, is quite another matter.)

Howard, for instance, might have tired faster than his companions on the swim out to the buoy. If so, he should have tapped his buddy to wait, while he inflated his CBJ and laid back to catch his breath. Since I had told the class never to exceed their limitations of strength or ability, he knew I wouldn't fail him for pausing for a rest. By not resting, Howard found himself gasping for breath, which was normal enough. But then he might have gotten worried that he wasn't getting enough breath and begun to hyperventilate. Then came the panic.

A second factor that could have caused Howard's problem is not feeling comfortable with a snorkle. A good snorkle allows a diver to get all the breath he needs, but because of its unfamiliarity, it often doesn't seem that way to a novice diver. He starts breathing in more than he really needs, afraid he's not getting enough. The more irregular the breathing becomes, the more anxiety he feels. When a diver hyperventilates, breathes so much that he can't control his breathing, he puts himself into panic. What a diver must do in that situation is to stop moving and concentrate on getting his breathing back into a normal rhythm. Putting his body at rest signals to the lungs: "Okay, now I'm helping out; I'm not doing anything that demands extra air, so you can slow down."

In Howard's case, however, I doubt that he started hyperventilating before he got to the buoy. When I asked if everyone was okay, he signalled that he was, and I didn't notice him having any difficulty before I headed down the line. Perhaps he was feeling the desire in his lungs to gasp for more air, but as long as I was there, he felt calm enough to overcome that urge. I was the control on him. And once I was gone, he slipped over the edge and began hyperventilating, then panicking.

When I resumed putting the remaining three-quarters of the class through its paces, everyone did fine. We completed the exercise and I signalled them to follow me to shore. Before I'd gone more than a few yards, I heard a woman calling for help. I looked around, and finally spotted her, about 30 yards off, wearing diving gear and floundering in the water. By this time, I figured that my class knew how to get to shore without me, so I sent them in and swam to the woman.

"I'm exhausted, I don't think I can make it," she told me.

"Did you throw your weight belt?" I asked.

"I don't want to lose it."

I wasn't about to debate the point with her; I ducked under the water and popped it off for her. Then I looked to see if her CBJ was fully inflated. It was. She wore one of those vests that has enough lift capacity to keep a parakeet floating maybe, but not an exhausted woman.

By now she was on her back, and I was towing her by her

tank valve. "My weight belt," she moaned, "what about my weight belt?"

"Hell with your weight belt."

I towed her in silence for a while, then she said, "I'm alright now, I can swim the rest of the way."

"Relax," I said. "Just lie back and enjoy the ride." There was no way I was going to release her now. I'd already invested time and energy in keeping her from drowning.

We reached the beach, and she became very gracious, full of appreciation for what I'd done. She was so gracious that she talked me into going back for her weight belt. I swam back out, searched the bottom until I found it, then brought it back in. I took my tanks off and knelt in the sand next to her, catching my breath. By this time *I* was nearing exhaustion, but I had to know something.

"Weren't you diving with a buddy?" I asked.

"I was with a diving class."

"You were with an instructor?"

"Yeah, the class is still out there," she said, pointing to a buoy and a diving flag.

Now all the strain and exhaustion changed into energy. I was angry. Her instructor had let her swim into shore by herself, as exhausted as she was! I had to see that guy. I left my tanks on the beach and swam out to the diving flag. Bubbles were coming up so they were right below me. I pulled on the line. Nothing happened. I pulled again. Still nothing. I began hauling the line up. Finally a diver came up.

"What do you want?" he demanded.

"Are you the instructor?"

"No, I'm the assistant."

"Get the instructor."

"What do you want him for?"

"Just get him."

When the instructor came up, I turned to the assistant and told him to get back down with the class. I didn't want him listening to what I had to say. "I thought you'd like to know that I just saved one of your students," I told the instructor.

"What do you mean?"

"You had a girl halfway to shore, almost drowning, and I had to pull her in. Now where the hell were you when one of your students was in trouble?"

"Oh, she told me she was tired and was going in. I would have gone with her, but she said she'd be alright. So I let her go."

"Look, you idiot, if someone's in trouble and tired you don't leave that person until she's standing on the shore with her equipment off!"

"I'll try to be more careful next time."

Unlike Howard, the girl I pulled in hadn't panicked. Her problem was simply exhaustion. Even good swimmers can overtire themselves. That's why I consider a proper control buoyancy jacket so important. If that instructor of hers had required proper CBJs, the girl would have had no problem. Even if she didn't want to part with her $20 weight belt, a CBJ with decent lift capacity could have kept her head well out of the water while she rested.

It must seem to the reader by now that I spend a good part of my time trying to convince people to throw their weight belts off when they're in trouble.

I do.

My longest day hadn't yet ended. Back on the beach, my class had assembled for its final exercise, a triangulated compass run. I put my tanks on again and led them toward the water. Then I noticed that I once more had four students, all with their tanks on, ready to go.

"Howard, what are you doing?"

"Oh, I feel a lot better now. I think I'll continue on with the course."

"Take your tank off, Howard, you're going no place near the water. If you're really that anxious to give it another try, you can sign up with another instructor and start again. But not today. Not with me. You're a hazard out there, and I'm just too tired for another emergency."

I ran the other three through the course with no further problems. Then I came back to my van, which I live in when I'm in Newport. A friend, Terry Conmy, was there and handed me a beer as I climbed in. The beer was cold and tasted very good. But I went to sleep before I could finish it.

CHAPTER 11

RESPECTING THE EQUIPMENT

One Sunday morning in spring, after having given a basic class its open-water checkout at the Quarry in Jersey, I stood on a rock overlooking the cold sparkling water, watching an instructor put his class through its paces. The class was from a maritime institution. I had seen the instructor earlier and knew he had to be a "mossback," an ex-Navy diver with old-fashioned ideas. He was hairy chested, chewed on a cigar whenever he wasn't in the water, had a "Mother" tattoo, and his head was nearly shaved.

The mossback had finished with the free diving portion of the instruction and brought his students back to the shore. Now he barked orders at them as they prepared to reenter the water, wearing full scuba gear. No one's wet suit seemed to fit. One student, who must have been six-foot-five and was built like a stork, wore a wet suit that came only halfway down his calves and left his wrists exposed to the water, which was 45 degrees. Their control buoyancy jackets must have been the cheapest money could buy, with lift capacities of 20 pounds at the most.

But the instructor wasn't worried about that. His interest centered on only one piece of equipment. "Alright, everyone over here on the double, get in line and pick up your knives. Everyone has to have a knife."

The crewcut assistant handed out knives that looked like

sabers. They had to be strapped to the students' legs. You would have thought they were preparing for a UDT assault across the Hudson River.

When they reentered the water, the students, freezing in their ill-fitted wet suits, performed poorly. The Quarry life guards, Steve and Richie, had already assisted more than one of the mossback's pupils, and now Steve floated a few feet away on his surfboard, ready for the next rescue.

The storklike student had trouble with the mask clearing exercise, and when he and the instructor came to the surface, the mossback yelled, "You're gonna do this right or get the hell out! You're holding up the rest of the group." The student's teeth were chattering and he was obviously flustered. A word of encouragement might have worked wonders. They descended again, and a few moments later the student popped to the surface in confusion, gagging and gasping for air. "Inflate your CBJ and lay back," the instructor yelled as he surfaced. The boy did so, and began sinking below the water. The lifeguard reached for him and pulled him to shore.

The instructor then gathered the class to move them to a different part of the Quarry for another exercise. But first he had a brief, inspirational message: "Now that Jones is out of here, I expect the rest of you to buckle down and get with the program. I don't want a repeat of that kind of performance. Okay, now, follow me." With that he stuck his regulator mouthpiece in his mouth and began swimming on the surface, doing a perfect Australian crawl. Emelio Bernabe, another instructor from our school, wandered by and I grabbed him and pointed to the mossback in the water. We both stared in amazement, then began cracking up. This old Navy diver was wasting his air by using his regulator instead of his snorkel, and wasting his energy by propelling himself with his arms instead of just using his fins.

Later on, back at the restaurant, I was in the men's room

when a couple of the mossback's students were changing. Still shivering, they congratulated each other for making it through the day. From over the partition to the women's room drifted the chatter of voices. Two women students, one from our school and one from an NASDS school in South Bay, Long Island, were talking: "Wasn't that great? I really had fun out there." "Well, I was scared at first, but then I saw how easy it was going to be and I relaxed. I can't wait to get out here again."

The two shivering young men stopped talking and glumly continued dressing.

The women had a good time because they were taught how to relax and to use their equipment properly. And they had the right equipment. The mossback's students were unfortunate enough to wind up in a class taught by an extreme example of the old style "gorilla" instructor.

The gorillas not only look upon scuba as a tough competition to be won by the strongest, they also downgrade the importance of the equipment used in diving. Any advances in scuba equipment are viewed with suspicion. Most of them learned to dive in the Navy years ago, when scuba gear was still primitive. Some still use the double-hose regulators they learned with. To them, any technological advance that makes scuba diving easier is something for sissies.

Many divers share this attitude. They feel threatened by machines or technology of any kind. I have seen this in some of my students. At first everyone feels uncomfortable wearing tanks and breathing through a regulator; it's a new and disconcerting experience to mechanize your breathing. I try to get students through this initial discomfort by making them understand just how scuba works. Most soon learn to adapt to the equipment, but some never learn to appreciate it. They're going to the bottom of the ocean to escape from the machine age, and they resent the idea of depending on machinery to do it. These are the people who tend to be fanatical about physical conditioning and swimming abilities, for they don't, at heart, trust the technology. And they refuse to learn about new devices that come on the market.

I feel very differently about the technology involved in scuba diving. I like to work with machines, so scuba equipment fascinates me. I understand how it operates, and I can take it apart and repair it; it is quite simple mechanically. And since this equipment enables me to travel to the underwater world, I appreciate it and want to learn as much about it as I can.

In scuba diving man doesn't rely on the machine to do everything for him; it's not like flying an airplane where man's brains make the decisions and the machine does all the work. With scuba, man and machine work so closely together that they virtually become one. A diver uses his tank and regulator for breathing, fins for propelling himself, mask for seeing, wet suit for warmth, and control buoyancy jacket for underwater mobility. He merges all these devices with his own skill and becomes a new type of amphibious being—a scuba diver.

The equipment our school provides each student always includes a CBJ, also known as a buoyancy compensator or BC. Some schools only teach the theory of the CBJ, and students don't have a chance to use them until their open-water checkouts. Because it's relatively new to the scuba world, many old-fashioned instructors categorize the CBJ as 'accessory equipment,' but our school teaches that it is essential equipment.

Through the fifties and most of the sixties, a diver had only limited means of dealing with a major problem: How could he use buoyancy as an aid rather than a hindrance to his mobility? A diver with a full tank and wet suit is more buoyant on the surface of the water than a swimmer in a bathing suit, because the rubberized material of the wet suit is composed of trapped nitrogen bubbles. The diver would have to exert great effort to fight his way down beneath the surface if he didn't wear a weight belt to reduce his positive buoyancy. A diver's buoyancy becomes more negative the deeper he goes because increased pressure squeezes his wet suit. At only one particular depth could the diver be neutrally buoyant. If he went deeper, he'd be negatively buoyant and would have to ascend by exerting muscle power against gravity. At any depth that was shallower than the point of neutral buoyancy, he'd have to push against his positive buoyancy to keep from floating to the surface. Scuba diving in the days before the CBJ required muscle power, exceptional swimming abilities and top conditioning. The compressed air vests that American divers wore at that time were strictly emergency devices to keep a diver afloat on the surface.

Then in the late sixties the control buoyancy jackets came to America from Europe. These jackets hooked up with the diver's compressed air supply and by push button, the diver could add more air to the vest, or bleed it off. That meant he could achieve neutral buoyancy, or negative or positive buoyancy, at any depth, by pushing a button. It was a major breakthrough in scuba diving and made the sport much easier.

The advantages of diving with a CBJ were so obvious that it caught on fast. But some still view the CBJ with suspicion. They didn't have the device when they learned how to dive, so they don't need it now and don't want their students to depend on CBJs. What if the vest fails, they ask, and you have to use good old leg power to get out of an emergency? Then you use good old leg power. But as long as the CBJ works, it helps the diver conserve his energy, which can be put to use in emergencies. Besides, our school always emphasizes that no student should rely on a CBJ in such a way that he overextends his own limitations.

The CO_2 cartridges with which the CBJs come equipped have aroused controversy in diving circles. Attached to the jacket, these metal cartridges (sometimes one but usually two) can be triggered in an emergency, immediately filling the CBJ with carbon dioxide and bringing the diver to the surface in a hurry. Many instructors distrust these cartridges and don't allow students to use them. They believe that when a diver is in a neutrally buoyant state, throwing his weight belt will lift him to the surface rapidly enough. Ascending any faster can be dangerous. Since the air in a diver's lungs expands as he ascends, a diver who neglects to exhale may wind up with an air embolism—air bubbles from overexpanded lungs forcing their way into the bloodstream.

When I was at Newport for my instructor's certification, I debated this point with some divers, mainly from the West Coast, who didn't use cartridges. I pointed out that, at least on the East Coast, we often dive negatively, to stay on the bottom when we're exploring wrecks, taking photographs or collecting lobsters. Then if a diver gets into trouble, throwing a weight belt might not be enough for a quick ascent. As for the danger of embolizing, the proper emergency rule of exhaling constantly is enough to avoid that danger.

When the water testing was finished one afternoon, I asked my water work proctor if I could give a demonstration of the CO_2 cartridges to prove my point. After he gave his okay, I gathered a group around me about 25 feet below the surface. I took the regulator out of my mouth, exhaling constantly, and triggered one of my 30-gram cartridges. It pulled me up so fast that I was halfway to the surface before I could get the weight belt off. Of course, I didn't embolize, which amazed some of the group.

The point is that the cartridges are there only for emergencies. And even if continuous exhaling doesn't totally eliminate the danger of embolizing, a diver is much better off with that danger when his air is cut off than the danger of not being able to reach the surface at all.

Some Caribbean resorts won't let divers use any kind of control buoyancy jackets. And I can sympathize with their position. They give very superficial diving courses to enable tourists to make easy, safe trips underwater with a guide. They don't have time to teach the proper use of a CBJ, and a novice diver might use one to ascend too rapidly without exhaling, and injure himself.

That's why proper instruction is so important. A diver has to know his equipment and how to use it properly or he can wind up in serious trouble. Pro dive shops have a code of ethics that prohibits the sale of underwater breathing equipment to customers without scuba certification cards. That distinguishes pro dive shops from sporting goods stores, which will sell to anyone, even by mail. Also, in a sporting goods store, you're likely to find a salesman who has never dived and only knows how to rattle off words from a manufacturer's catalog. A diver who goes into a pro dive shop will be waited on by someone who knows the equipment and has a commitment to the sport.

That someone might be me. The instructors in our school also serve as "counsellors" for the dive shop and are paid commissions for equipment they sell. I've heard instructors from other organizations complain about this practice. Some instructor, they say, could oversell, convince a trusting student to buy more than he needs. In theory, that danger might exist. But I've never seen it happen. Instructors know their students' needs better than anyone else and are therefore in a better position to advise them.

It's important to me that a fellow diver, especially a student of mine, buys the piece of equipment that's right for him, and that's not necessarily the highest priced item. I don't encourage him to buy the cheapest equipment on the market, either, because if he's serious about diving he'll just wind up replacing it anyway.

Recently, someone came into the shop and asked my opinion on whether he should buy a 72-cubic-foot tank or a pair of 45s. I wouldn't give him a flat answer, but spelled out to him the advantages and disadvantages of each. The two 45s give a total of 18 more cubic feet of air. I wear them, not just for the extra air but also because I find them more comfortable on my back. However, on a 72 he can get a depth-compensated, adjustable reserve so the amount of air in his reserve isn't reduced by increased pressure when he goes deeper. The 45s are also more expensive. I told him all I knew, gave him the benefit of my experience, then let him tell me what he wanted.

Often I'm asked what equipment I use. Everything I have I consider the very best for my purposes, but it's not always the latest piece of equipment or the most expensive. I use steel tanks instead of aluminum, for instance. Since I give my tanks good maintenance, I have no problem with rusting. Aluminum tanks are lighter, and that helps when you're lugging them around. But it doesn't mean very much in the water, since you have to carry extra weights to compensate; and you have to lug those weights around too. Also, the valves on steel tanks still mate better than they do on aluminum ones. Some of the new equipment on the market combines two or more elements of scuba gear: tanks, buoyancy control, weights, wet or dry suits. I've tried them all, and so far I've stuck to my separate equipment as best for me and the kind of diving I do. While I never distrust new developments as such, I don't automatically assume that something new must work better.

When selling equipment, one thing I always emphasize to the customer is the guarantee. Not only should the guarantee be comprehensive, it also should be one that the dealer can cover. If something breaks, the customer should be able to bring it to the place he bought it and have them replace or repair it. Some dealers delegate to Cougar and other shops the authority to decide whether damage was caused by negligence or product malfunction. We make the decision, repair or replace the piece, and the manufacturer backs us up. If the manufacturer insists that he must decide, that means the customer has to ship the piece of equipment to the factory which may be thousands of miles away; as a courtesy, we'll box it and ship it for him, but that's all we can do for the customer.

The most important piece of equipment a diver buys is the regulator. If it's made by a name manufacturer, it's almost sure to be safe, and even lesser known companies make devices that are usually reliable. But there are exceptions, especially some imports that can be found in shops here and there.

Years ago, when I made my basic certification dive at Lake Minnewaska, the school wasn't as strict on the equipment requirements as they are now. Several of us were at the edge of the lake, preparing our equipment, when one of the students turned on his tank; we could all hear a hissing sound. I went over to help out, believing it must be a problem with the O-ring in the valve. Maybe some sand got into it. I turned off the tank, took the regulator off and checked the O-ring. It looked alright, but I cleaned it, turned it around and put it back in. When he turned the tank on again, it still hissed. Just then one of the instructors walked over, looked at the regulator and asked, "Where'd you get that?"

The student had bought the cheapest model in a sporting goods store. The instructor had seen this brand regulator before. "Let me show you something," he said.

He took the regulator off the tank and put one hand on the hose and the other on the first stage, which attaches to the tank valve. Then he very gently pulled, and the hose came off the first stage. The hose wasn't screwed in; it was held to the metal only by a weak band clamp. The instructor wouldn't let him in the water with that regulator, so I did my checkout dive first, then lent him mine.

Imagine being in 100 feet of water, getting your regulator hose snagged on something and having it pull apart. Now you have no air and 100 feet of water to deal with. If a diver wants to avoid this kind of trouble, he has an obligation to learn about his equipment. However mistrustful of technology he may be, he should force himself to understand the simple mechanical devices that enable him to breathe underwater. Otherwise he would be better off sticking to free diving.

A diver who cares about his equipment has his tank inspected every year, a procedure called Visual Inspection Protection, or VIP. According to federal law, a scuba cylinder has to be hydrostatically tested every five years, to see that it safely measures up to its rated pressure. But if saltwater gets inside the tank, it can become rusted and dangerously weakened well inside of five years. Our shop won't fill a diver's tank if he doesn't have a sticker on it that says it has been visually inspected within the past year. Some divers complain that this policy is a ripoff. Actually, it's a good example of the industry's self regulation since the policy doesn't make much money for the shop.

In a visual inspection, the tank is depressurized, the valve removed and the inside of the tank inspected with a light for any signs of rust, corrosion, moisture or foreign matter. Moisture can be evaporated easily enough, and rust and corrosion can be removed by putting an abrasive grit in the tank and tumbling it on rollers. Eddie Mayer, one of our instructors who does repairs and inspections for the shop, says that he has taken up to a gallon of water out of tanks. He has found candy and gum in the valves and a ladybug inside a tank. Once he discovered a crumpled note with a telephone number on it. He called the number and found out it was a prison, though what connection it had with the scuba tank he never learned.

Eddie tells one story about a diver who had a close involvement with our shop. "He had been getting a little sick after about the third dive of the day," Eddie says, "but he blamed it on just being tired. Finally I convinced him to bring his tank in for a VIP. I opened it up, and it looked like a rock garden in there, it was so rusty. No wonder he was getting sick. He had to throw the tank away. And this was the guy who was doing the shop's hydrostatic testing at the time."

You don't have to be a mechanical expert to be a good scuba diver. You don't even have to accept the role of technology in our society. But you do have to care for, and respect, your scuba equipment. Underwater man is a new creature to our modern era, a blending of man's technological genius with his age-old adventurous spirit—and both elements are important.

CHAPTER 12

GHOSTS IN THE DEPTHS

When you dive into a wreck, you travel into another dimension of time. Roman galley or modern freighter, men once lived in it, operated it and cared about it. When it sank, it departed from human history; to men, the ship has died.

But here it is, looming before you, a ghost existing in a world apart from all human purposes. It is not dead; it has been reincarnated into something else. It serves a new function in the life of the planet. The hull, built to keep the ship above water, lies broken in the sand, covered with living coral. Moray eels, sting rays, parrot fish and trumpet fish have made the former ship their home. The dead ship has brought life to the area.

It's as though Mother Nature decided that men had enough ships, but inhabitants of the watery world needed a new housing development, so she blew up a storm, sank the ship and gave to fish what was once man's. The shipbuilders never realized they were building the heart of a reef for fish, something that would serve marine life for many more eons than it would serve man.

I drop slowly onto the mahogany deck of what was a magnificent turn-of-the-century yacht. I can see the dining salon, built to the lavish tastes of a very rich man. Here, perhaps, business deals were discussed, and plots were laid to make rich men richer. Champagne must have been sipped. Now the last owner of the yacht, if he still lives, speaks of it in the past tense. But the dining salon goes on serving. A chain of life, simple to complex, all feeding on one another, fills the salon with more life than it had in its days above the sea. I see lobsters scuttling about whose ancestors were once served thermidor in that very room.

I always feel at home underwater, but I know I am an alien. This is not man's any more. It has been claimed by another world.

No one knows the numbers of ships that have been wrecked, but even the estimates are staggering. The Michigan waters of the Great Lakes hold some 6000 known wrecks. Diamond Shoals, off Cape Hatteras lighthouse in North Carolina, is the graveyard for 3000 ships. In World War II, German U-boats sank 2603 Allied and neutral merchant ships. Because of wartime secrecy, most Americans were unaware of the many ships that went down in flames within our territorial waters.

Divers regularly visit a number of these wrecks. Wreck diving fascinates many scuba enthusiasts despite—or because of—the fact it can be very difficult and very dangerous diving.

In July of 1974, I went on a wreck dive with Don Arrington, the New York City homicide detective who teaches underwater photography at our school; Leroy Bonaparte, who looks like a black Buddha and works for the City University system; and Terry Conmy, who works in educational videotape, a recent student of mine in whom I had taken a special interest. We left from Brielle, New Jersey, on the *Bottom Time,* a 45-foot boat operated by Charlie Stratton, one of the top wreck-diving captains on the East Coast. As usual, Charlie's boat was covered with old batteries, rusted tools, pieces of machines, junk he has brought up from wrecks, swearing to make use of someday.

Charlie's navigation is as uncanny as his boat is messy. Once I went with him to dive a wreck he had discovered and whose location he was very wary about keeping to himself. He maneuvered around the area for an hour, refusing to head for the right location until a fishing boat in the distance disappeared over the horizon. Wrecks are prime fishing areas, and one that hasn't yet been fished would be a real boon to a fishing-boat captain, most of whom know Charlie's boat and his business. When the fishing boat left, Charlie turned toward his secret wreck and a few minutes later dropped his anchor right on its boiler, as if he could see some landmark in the waves invisible to the rest of us.

On this warm July day, we were diving two wrecks, heading first for the *Arundo,* a 5079-ton Dutch cargo carrier built in 1930. On April 28, 1942, at 5:00 A.M., the *Arundo* left New York Harbor carrying locomotive engines strapped to the deck, plus other cargo below. The ship was bound for Alexandria, Egypt, but four and a half hours out of port the *Arundo* was spotted by a German U-boat. The torpedo struck below the waterline, under the bridge on the starboard side. Hold number two flooded almost immediately, and the ship began to list rapidly. The 43-man crew didn't have to be told what had happened. They scrambled for the lifeboats and rafts, and some, seeing how fast their ship was sinking, just dove off the side. In five minutes, the *Arundo* began to slide beneath the waves. As her deck tilted steeply, a locomotive strapped to the deck broke loose and crashed into the sea where a number of the crew were swimming. Four were killed. A destroyer, the U.S.S. *Lea,* sighted the sinking ship from six miles away and picked up the survivors.

The *Arundo* must have been carrying some valuable cargo besides the locomotives. After the war, in November 1945, a major salvage attempt was made, despite the fact the *Arundo*

Wreck-diving captain Charlie Stratton shows off another piece of junk he has salvaged. *(Photo by Don Arrington)*

lies in 130 feet of water. The salvage attempt failed, and some years later the wreck was rediscovered by scuba divers.

By the time we reached the waters above the *Arundo*, the swells were running four feet, and Terry began to feel uneasy. I suggested that her stomach would probably settle down once she was in the water. We all put on our wet suits and prepared to dive. Few places in the world are hotter than the inside of a wet suit on a hot day before you get into the water. By the time we did, Terry was hyperventilating. I told her to relax, enjoy the coolness of the ocean and get her breathing back to normal. We hung on the line for several minutes, while Don and Leroy went on ahead. When Terry's breathing steadied, we headed down the line.

Wrecks off the Jersey coast seem more mysterious than those found in the Caribbean; the murkiness of the North Atlantic imparts an eerie mood to a dive. I knew that down there, through the darkness, lay the broken wreck of a ship, but all I could see was eight feet of line ahead of me, disappearing into nothingness.

Transparent, pulsating jellyfish, with long tentacles, floated all around us as we descended. The water temperature was 60 degrees, but I could see a thermocline shimmering below us. The icy chill knifed through our wet suits as we dropped into a layer of 45-degree water. It's as drastic a change as going from a hot beach into a cool surf.

We were almost on top of the wreck before we could see it. Few shipwrecks lie neatly intact on the bottom. Like most, the *Arundo* consisted of huge broken masses of twisted steel. I led the way with my Giddings Felgen light extended in front of me, and we moved along the hull, the only clear landmark in the dark waters. We swam over a jumble of metal that, after a second, I recognized as one of the locomotives the *Arundo* had carried. We passed a stretch where the entire ship was split in two. The rusting steel hull had jagged, gaping holes but was alive with fish. Scattered everywhere along the bottom were tires, engine blocks, truck differentials and many other pieces of machinery I couldn't identify.

Near the bow I glanced up and I didn't like what I saw: A trawler's net had caught on the wreck, torn free of the trawler and now covered the entire area above us. It was steel, so I guessed it to be Russian; Americans use rope, which doesn't present nearly the problem to divers that steel does. I knew we could work our way out from underneath the net. A wrong move, though, could tangle one of us in that steel. I worried about Terry. I didn't want her first wreck dive to be ruined by the frightening sight of a steel net seeming to enclose us, so I kept pointing out things on the bottom as I worked our way from underneath the net. We joined up with Don and Leroy, then we had to head up. Since we had a second dive coming up, we wanted to avoid decompression. At 130 feet you don't have much bottom time within the no-decompression limits.

With his usual ease, Charlie found the second wreck, an old one that no one has been able to identify. Terry's seasickness had returned and when she suited up again, she became sick to her stomach. Don and Leroy had already gone down the line. I knew Terry had better not dive this time, and I helped her out of her wet suit. My company wouldn't be very welcome in her seasick condition, and I didn't want to give up my dive. I decided to hop in the water, head on down the line and catch up with the others.

No one has to tell me that diving without a buddy is very dangerous business, especially on a wreck dive. I'd told students, such as Terry, that often enough. But I planned to buddy up with Don and Leroy on the bottom.

The visibility was about eight feet as I reached the end of the line, 90 feet down. The wooden skeleton of the old sailing ship rose out of the sandy bottom, disappearing into the murk above. I could find no sign of Don and Leroy. They could have gone either right or left. I guessed right, since most people tend to go to their right given a choice. I moved along the ghostly ribs, then I thought I saw a light flicker ahead. I kicked a little harder to catch up.

Suddenly I was pulled back. Something was tugging on me. I looked down at my legs and fins and saw they had gotten tangled in fishing line. A popular spot for party boats to fish, the wreck had over the years captured many monofilament lines that clung like a spider's web to the wooden ribs.

I wasn't worried, though. I just pulled out my knife, cut through the lines and started swimming again. A sharper tug —I couldn't move! I still hadn't freed myself. I felt a quiver in my stomach. I do not scare easily, but all of us have our private fears and dreads. And to me, being trapped is the stuff of nightmares. I fought down the fear. Then I looked back and saw that the lines were all around me. I realized that my weight belt was caught so I took it off, laying it across my knees so I wouldn't lose it in the sand. I cut through the lines on the belt, then cut the lines clinging to me. I put the weight belt back on, started moving again—and got pulled back again! My God, I was still trapped!

My lungs demanded more air and a chill cut me to the bone, signs that fear was getting to me. A diver should always take four or five seconds underwater to gain control of himself in a tight situation, to think before he even starts to react. If he reacts too fast, without thinking things through, he can make it worse.

I knelt on the sand, fighting down surges of panic. Calm down! Think! Concentrate! I looked at my gauges, and remembered a teacher I once had who taught me to look at my watch before answering a difficult question; that way you get an extra few seconds to think it over. My air was fine, but when I glanced at my decompression meter I saw it was moving toward the red zone. If it reached red, I'd have to take the time to decompress on the way up. I might not have enough air for that, especially at the rate I was using it up now.

I stopped looking at the meter; it would only make me speed up too much and I'd just get myself tangled worse. Since my tanks were caught this time, I did a doff-and-don, an emergency procedure I'd taught every student I had, but never had occasion to use myself in a real situation. I loosened my left shoulder buckle and waist buckle and slid the tanks in front of me, still keeping the regulator in my mouth.

I could see the tangles of line now and I had to decide: Do I separate myself from the tanks in 90 feet of water and do a buoyant free ascent? Or do I take the time to try to cut them free? I decided to stay with the tanks. I dragged them as far away from the wreck as I could, pulled out the knife again and started cutting. I didn't worry about all the knots and tangles around the tanks; I chopped a couple of feet away from the tanks, at the filament between the tanks and the wreck. I had to break that umbilical cord tying me to the wreck that loomed like a haunted ship a few feet away in the murky water.

But I was working coolly now. That flash of panic had only been brief. It now looked as though I'd cut myself free. I slipped my arms through the straps and pulled the tanks over my head. After I strapped myself in, I began swimming, and kept swimming! I suppressed a surge of joy: "Of course, you're free, it was just a minor annoyance, don't get so excited." Then I saw Don and Leroy's light ahead. I swam up to them and when they saw me I gave such an emphatic "okay" sign that Don looked puzzled. "Sure you're okay," he seemed to be saying, "who said you weren't?" I signalled that we three were now buddies. My decompression meter still hadn't moved into the red zone, but then Leroy's regulator began to honk—signalling he was running out of air.

We headed for the line, then up. For a reason neither Don

nor Leroy could understand at the time, I did some flips on the way.

If I'd been with a buddy, becoming trapped in monofilament fishing lines wouldn't have even been cause to skip a pulse beat. My buddy could have cut me out of them. So this experience reinforced what I had always taught my classes: Having a buddy, or thinking you have a buddy nearby, isn't good enough; your buddy must be right there with you, an arm's length away, to be any good to you.

That same summer off Jersey, a diver I knew made the mistake of diving without a buddy, though others were with him on a wreck dive. He made a second, even more serious mistake. He entered the wreck without a lifeline. He never came up. By the time the others noticed he had disappeared, it was too late.

Entering a wreck is very tricky business. As soon as a diver

The coral-encrusted spar I'm examining is on the Bermuda wreck *Minnie Bresleur,* which sank in 1873. *(Photo by Don Arrington)*

steps inside, his fins, exhaust bubbles, his slightest movement stir up all the silt and rust. Those few feet of visibility the diver had are gone. He can see literally nothing. But he remembers where the entry point was, just a couple of feet away. He moves back toward it, and feels only a wall. Finding a way out of a wreck isn't like finding a way out of a non-wrecked ship; the diver keeps running into tangled masses of metal, collapsed walls, jagged edges. He panics, his air consumption goes up. He screams with no one to hear him. . . .

Treasure lures many to ship wrecks. And fabulous treasures have been found on the bottom of the seas. Spanish galleons have yielded millions in gold. Many Spanish treasure ships were sunk by the storms of the Caribbean and the Atlantic. Certainly many, if not most, are still to be found. But these treasures do not reveal themselves to amateur

This split in a wreck's hull may be wide enough to enter, but without a lifeline it's too dangerous. *(Photo by Joseph Payne)*

fortune seekers. What the treasure hunter has to look for in the clear Caribbean waters is not a slightly battered galleon resting on a sandy bottom, but an odd looking clump of coral, or a series of mounds near a reef. The treasure hunter has to mount a major expedition that requires long patient effort with sophisticated tools to find out if there is indeed a treasure to be recovered. And recovering it may take years of careful work.

An experienced wreck diver knows that he'll never find a treasure trove of gold doubloons, but he dreams of another kind of treasure—perhaps a ship's brass bell. Eddie Mayer, my friend and fellow instructor at the Skin Diving School of New York, is the epitome of the wreck diver, subdivision: scavenger. Eddie, a balding chap with a pleasant and easy manner, got his certification back in 1963. Though he says it was the movie *Frogman,* rather than *Captain Kidd* or *Treasure Island* that turned him on to diving, he has been diving wrecks for more than a dozen years. When Eddie wreck dives, usually off the Jersey or Long Island coast, he enters the water with a hacksaw, chisel, hammer and other assorted tools, plus a large nylon bag. "If it's shiney, it comes up with me," he says.

I once dived the *Montana* with Eddie and Buzzie Driscoll, a friend of ours. The *Montana,* a large sailing ship, sank in 75 feet of water off Block Island about 1830. Only the cross-beams and curved rib sections remain intact, though many pieces of metal and assorted artifacts can be found scattered in the sand nearby.

We went on a crowded dive boat, and when we reached the site about 40 divers entered the water. They bumped into each other, kicked up the sand and almost ruined the peaceful feeling of being under the sea. But the three of us planned to outlast the others. We came up from the first dive, got new tanks and went down again, and this time only half the crowd was there. Since we were the most experienced divers on the boat, we used less air than the others, and the third time we went down, we were the only three in the water. A bottom current had started and by the time we were halfway down the line, it had swept out all the silt and sand that had been kicked up. It was as if a curtain had lifted. We could see the whole wreck spread open before us, graceful and beautiful even in its decayed state. We let go of the line and just floated into the wreck. I was filling my nylon bag with brass nails and zinc plates. Buzzie got hold of some copper pipes. But Eddie moved like a harvesting machine, plucking up pieces of brass from the sand as if he instinctively knew where to find them, though he used no metal detector.

Eddie has taught me his techniques for scavenging, and I've begun to build up a pretty fair collection of artifacts from wrecks I've dived, though not as impressive as Eddie's. He has a wall in his living room filled with brass plaques, spikes, lanterns and other objects he has brought up. Eddie saves his personal treasures, but I know another wreck diver who makes several hundred a year selling his finds to dealers, and still manages to build up an impressive collection of his own.

Last year I was diving the wreck of the *Maine,* a steel hulled freighter, with Eddie. I had just come down after getting another tank and I spotted Eddie, struggling with a large brass valve. His vest was fully inflated but he was going nowhere. I came over, inflated mine and between the two of us we managed to bring the hulk to the surface, another souvenir for Eddie's wall.

Wreck scavengers learn the various ways water conditions affect a wreck, and the different rates at which various materials deteriorate. Cold freshwater like that in the Great Lakes is the best preserver of ship wrecks. Lake wrecks often have wooden hulls intact after a century underwater. Next best is saltwater in northern regions, such as the Northeast Coast. In the tropics, almost everything from a ship quickly becomes encrusted with coral, unless it is buried in the sand.

Mickey Whalen finds a small coral tree growing from the *Rhone* off the British Virgin Islands. *(Photo by Jim Gott)*

Portholes make prize souvenirs, but this one is still attached to the wreck. *(Photo by Joseph Payne)*

On wrecks that date from the 19th Century, wood planking is usually eaten away by teredo worms in warm waters or rotted away by the saltwater in colder waters, but wooden beams and ribs often remain. Steel, iron and silver become encrusted and corroded quickly in saltwater, and if the object is small it's sometimes difficult to tell these metals from a rock except by shape. Gold, lead, brass, copper and glass usually suffer only superficial damage, even when they've been down for a century. Some deposits or corrosion may form, and brass and copper often turn slightly green.

When a diver brings up an artifact from a wreck, he has to know what to do with it. Drying out and contact with the air can damage the object further. The first rule is to keep the object wet. Fresh water is preferable for everything except coral-encrusted objects, which should be kept in salt water. To clean the surfaces of iron and steel, soak them in Rustoline; for copper and brass, use a solution of Rochelle salt.

A free diver examines an anchor from a 16th-Century wreck off Central America. *(Photo by Jim Gott)*

Terry Conmy complains that the typewriter's keys are rusty. *(Photo by Jim Gott)*

Sometimes a high-power hose or sandblaster should be used as a first step in removing corrosion and encrustations.

To prevent further corrosion, it's often a good idea to remove salts by boiling metal objects in a sodium hydroxide bath. An oven can be used to dry the metal, after this desalting bath. A further step for preventing new corrosion is to coat the object with plastic or wax.

Then on your mantel will rest a prize of your diving, something built by men, lost to the sea and now again returned to human society.

I don't feel I've robbed the sea by bringing up these artifacts. I've just completed a strange cycle.

CHAPTER 13

DANGERS DOWN BELOW

I teach *safe* scuba diving. By the time a student finishes my course, he or she will know the potential dangers of diving and how to avoid them, and will be well drilled in all the emergency procedures.

I stress the dangers, but I try not to exaggerate them. I don't want to frighten students or make them feel they're showing death defying courage in taking up the sport. I want my students to enjoy scuba, and to do that they have to learn to feel relaxed and confident about it. Scuba is a safe sport —*if* the diver approaches it with the right attitude and the right training.

The University of Rhode Island has been doing studies in scuba safety, and the statistics they've compiled show scuba diving to have an impressive safety record. With about two million divers in the United States, one million of whom are active, less than 600 scuba deaths occurred in the recent five-year period covered by the study. The number of scuba divers has been increasing over this period, but the total number of deaths per year have remained relatively steady, meaning a declining death rate. Compared with most sports, from football to swimming to backpacking, scuba's record is a good one.

Scuba diving, however, is a sport with more than its share of hazards. Only by recognizing this has the scuba world been able to compile a good safety record. It's more than coincidence that the declining death rate correlates with the increasing percentage of divers who've gone through a national certification program, plus increasing standards of self regulation by the industry. If scuba diving were a self-taught sport, with no national organizations giving scuba courses and promoting safety, I'd hate to see what the fatality rates would be.

Part of safety in any area is being sensible and avoiding potential dangers. If everyone were always sensible, a lot of the worries of the world would pass away, but few of us always are. And even the best divers do reckless things once in a while.

Take Bobby McCormick, for instance. An ex-Coast Guard diver, Bobby looks like an old salt. His chest is almost as big as his belly, he stands a little under six feet, and he wears a perpetually bemused expression on his bearded face. Bobby, who has often been my diving buddy, tells of a tight situation he got himself into when spearfishing with another friend on a reef off Spanish Hondorus:

"We must have been in the water forty minutes, diving at about a hundred and twenty-five feet, when I saw my buddy take off down the side of the reef. I couldn't figure out if he was in trouble and didn't know which way he was going or if he just saw something very good down there that he had to get a look at. So I started after him, checking my depth gauge as I went. We hit two hundred feet, then two twenty, then two thirty. Finally he turned around to meet me at two hundred and forty feet. I pulled up next to him, and he seemed alright—not narcing. I didn't feel I was narcing, either.

"My depth gauge went to two hundred and fifty feet, and I was intrigued with being so deep. I decided to go the extra ten feet and 'peg' the gauge out. I started heading down, when my buddy caught me by my fin. I looked back, and he made the sign, drawing a finger across his throat, for having run out of air. Why the hell he hadn't started up when he went on reserve, I couldn't figure out. Maybe he *was* narcing. But, no problem. I had a Mark VII regulator with an octopus system. I gave him the extra regulator mouthpiece, so we were both breathing off my tank.

"Just then my Mark VII began to honk, meaning that I was going on reserve. I knew we wouldn't have much air to breathe at that depth, but I didn't realize just how fast it would run out. I started inflating my CBJ for the ascent and heard: Honnnkkk . . . The honker faded, and now I was out of air too. I said to myself, 'How could I have been dumb enough to get into this spot—out of air 240 feet down?' But I kept my cool. I was holding my speargun and even then I wasn't about to drop it. I reached down with my right hand and pulled one CO_2 cartridge, then switched the speargun to my right hand and pulled the other cartridge with my left.

"I had often told my classes that Boyle's Law means that no matter how deep you are, you can keep exhaling all the way up, because the air in your lungs keeps expanding, and you'll feel no need to breath in. Of course, I had never tried it from two hundred and forty feet, but the air just kept coming and coming. I kept my eye on my buddy and he seemed to be doing alright, too. We broke the surface like a couple of missiles and checked each other out.

"Then we had the second part of the emergency procedure to get through: We had to get new tanks and get back down fast in order to decompress, and we were away from the boat. We blew our whistles for the boat to pick us up. When it came near, we began yelling, 'Tanks, tanks!' They must have thought it was very funny and yelled back to us, 'You're welcome, you're welcome!' But they did have the tanks ready for us and we quickly descended for our decompression. Neither of us wound up with the bends, fortunately.

"I tell the story now and laugh about it, but every once in a while, I think about what could have happened. . . ."

The deeper a diver is, the more dramatic the emergency. But that doesn't mean that a diver is less likely to run into trouble on the surface. In fact, diving is like piloting a plane: The takeoff and landing—entry and exit from the water—are especially dangerous situations. I watched a horrifying example of this out at Shinnecock Inlet several years ago. I was sitting on the rock jetty, talking with another diver. A few others were on the jetty, including some fishermen and a conservation officer. The other diver, who had been gazing out over the water as we talked, interrupted our conversation to say, "Look at that fool! He's going to get himself hurt!" I looked where he was pointing and saw a lone diver swimming on the surface toward the jetty.

We'd been diving the jetty together that day, though the water was rough, so neither of us had to tell the other what the diver was doing wrong. Exiting on a rock jetty is very difficult because of the waves that constantly slap against it. To avoid as much wave action as possible, the diver should not approach from the surface but from underwater, then climb up carefully, rock by rock, holding on to the rock while a wave crashes over it.

We watched apprehensively as the diver neared the jetty. A receding wave pushed him back and swept him up onto the peak of the next oncoming wave. He was held there momentarily, then hurtled with the wave against the rocks. He hit hard, high up the water line, and lay there motionless. Before we could move, two fishermen rushed down to help him, then called over the conservation officer. By the time we reached the diver, I knew it was bad. He'd been wearing his tank too loosely, and when he crashed onto the rocks, his tank kept going, and the tank valve had smashed into the back of his skull. We helped the conservation officer lift him and bring him away from the waves, but we could tell that he was already dead.

It's hard enough watching someone die, but it's even worse when you know the death could easily have been avoided. If only someone had taught that diver the proper way to dive a jetty . . . If only he had put his equipment on correctly before the dive . . . If only he'd been diving with a buddy who knew a little more than he did about jetty diving, or at least could have checked to see if his tank straps were tight enough.

I tell my students that almost all diving accidents can be traced to the diver's negligence, to his ignorance, or to panic. Anyone can panic, but unfamiliar dangers cause that reaction far more often than known dangers. If my students are able to remember what they've been taught about a particular bad situation, they're in much better position to control their emotional reactions to it. One thing I know about the divers I've taught: No matter what difficulty they find themselves in, at least they'll have been taught how to deal with it. And unless they've totally ignored my advice, they'll be wearing all the proper equipment, including decompression meters and pressure gauges.

The National Association of Underwater Instructors has been running an international diving accident investigation project, and they've found that 35 to 40 percent of the diving deaths in Southern California over an eight year period might not have occurred if the diver had been using a gauge that told him how much air he had in his tank at all times. A pressure gauge is far safer than just relying on a J-valve, which allows the diver to go on reserve before he totally runs out of air. All too often the diver forgets to put the reserve lever in the proper position, or the lever gets knocked down by accident into the reserve position. Then when the diver runs out of air and tries to pull open the reserve, he finds the rod already down, and he's totally out of air.

Some types of diving present far more dangers than others: night diving; extreme depth; extreme cold; bad surface conditions; places where the diver doesn't have free access to the surface such as in caves, under ice or inside wrecks. If a diver chooses these situations, he should at least be aware of the risks.

I tell my students that no diver has to exceed the no-decompression limits or venture into a difficult diving situation. Diving isn't a competitive sport, and the most enjoyable dives are those in clear, calm and temperate waters—and no deeper than 100 feet, for most everything worth seeing is found above that depth.

Of course, neither my students nor I always take this advice. And by pushing the limits of safe diving and venturing into dangerous areas, some of them will find themselves in tight spots. But a competent diver, and I hope I can include all my students in that category, will have the knowledge and training to cope with the situation.

Knowing you have no one to blame but yourself when you're in a jam underwater isn't nearly as comforting as knowing how to get out of it.

CHAPTER 14

JAWS I HAVE KNOWN

In 1974, students who had read the book started asking the question: "Hey, Jimmy, what about sharks? Aren't they dangerous to divers, especially off Long Island?"

Now everyone who hasn't read it has seen the movie, or at least all my students have. "I know *Jaws* is all fiction, Jimmy, but what happens if you're diving and a shark with an empty stomach comes along?"

Jaws didn't invent any phobias about sharks; it played on fears man has had since the first prehistoric sailors. For the shark is a powerful, graceful and terrifying creature. With rows upon rows of dagger teeth and eyes that light up like a cat's at night, the shark hunts and kills so efficiently that evolution has hardly changed its design for 300 million years. Few sights in nature can evoke the horror of a shark-feeding frenzy. Jacques Cousteau wrote in *The Living Sea* of "the hatred of sharks that lies so close under the skin of a sailor." The hatred and fear stem from knowledge that sharks have often attacked and killed men without seeming provocation.

And yet, sharks do not pose nearly the danger that old legends or current movies would have you believe. In general, the more man learns about the sea's creatures, the less fearsome they seem. This applies to the shark, though not entirely.

I tell my students that I've been diving for 17 years, often in shark infested waters, and no shark teeth have marked my body. A diver only rarely encounters a shark, and when he does, the shark almost never shows any eagerness to attack. Much of what we have heard about sharks is myth. One fable that has been repeated in an Air Force survival manual, for instance, is that a drop of blood in the water will attract frenzied sharks from miles around. Experiments have disproved this. In one, rodents in various states of mutilation were thrown into shark tanks. The rodents' blood had no affect on the sharks; only when rodents' stomach juices were added to the water were the sharks attracted. Rescuers going to help profusely bleeding shark-attack victims are almost never attacked themselves, which shows that the presence of blood in the water doesn't by itself trigger the sharks' ferocity.

Another myth is that sharks attack humans simply for the sake of a meal. In fact, an analysis of a Shark Attack File once maintained by the Smithsonian Institution for the Office of Naval Research showed that only a small percent of shark attacks on humans seem to be motivated by hunger. Evidence of this is the fact that most victims of shark attacks survive to tell about it; the shark makes its attack but doesn't eat its prey.

Despite the exaggerations and the myths, however, sharks are dangerous creatures. They didn't acquire their reputations mainly by looking fierce and menacing, as did barracuda. They don't usually attack humans, but sometimes they do. Though much study has been done on sharks since World War II, we still understand very little about their behavior. We don't know just what causes them to attack, or refrain from attacking. We call their behavior "unpredictable," perhaps only because we don't understand them well enough to predict it.

Part of the problem in studying sharks is that there are 250 to 300 species, with almost as many patterns of behavior.

Some are less than a foot long, others range up to 60 feet. Some species including the whale shark, which is the largest, are totally harmless to men, but others have earned their reputations for viciousness.

Sharks are distinguished from other fish by a number of common characteristics. All have cartilage skeletons rather than bones, and, unlike boney fish, they have no swim bladders. They have to keep constantly on the move, or their negative buoyancy will cause them to sink. Instead of scales, sharks have a rough hide. Some species lay eggs and others bear their young live, but all species reproduce by sexual intercourse. The male is equipped with two penises, inappropriately called claspers. Why the extra penis, no one seems to know.

Some things are known about shark behavior. One valuable piece of information is that before launching an attack, a shark usually assumes a distinct posture: With arched back, it sways its head from side to side. A shark's feeding instincts can be triggered by vibrations as well as by smells. Probably thinking it means a fish in distress, therefore a potential meal, the shark hones in on the source of the vibration. A human splashing away as he swims on the surface might seem to a shark like a wounded fish. This is why divers have always felt safer from sharks than a swimmer on the surface—provided that the diver isn't spearfishing and carrying a string of dying fish.

Over the years many defenses against sharks have been tried, some based on superstition, others on experience or scientific experiment. Hans Hass, an early underwater explorer and spearfisherman, discovered that yelling at sharks seemed to frighten them off. He also found that he could chase them off by swimming directly at them. He may just have been lucky, though. Subsequent studies have shown that swimming at a shark can trigger its sense of territoriality and cause it to attack.

One diver, Walt Starck, designed and tested a black and white banded wet suit that he believes deters sharks; the bands resemble the markings on the sea snake, a poisonous fish sharks know not to attack. The U.S. Navy tested the suit without success, but Starck claims that the tests were poorly designed.

Shark repellents have been developed for years, but none so far has proved to be consistently effective. Recently, though, Dr. Eugenie Clark, a marine biologist, discovered what she believes could be a shark repellent that works very well. Experiments she conducted showed that a poisonous fluid produced by a Red Sea flatfish gave attacking sharks an instant case of lockjaw. Since the substance seems harmless to humans, the hope is that it could be synthesized and used as an anti-shark lotion.

If it ever reaches the market, divers will probably be prime customers. Though sharks aren't encountered too often by divers, most of us who've been into scuba for years have met some of the beasts. I've known few long-time divers who didn't have some shark stories they were eager to tell.

Eddie Mayer was spearfishing once, diving on reserve and carrying his catch on a stringer, when he looked down and saw a shark below him—just as his air ran out and he got a cramp. But the shark displayed no interest in Eddie or his problems.

John Schuch, the owner of the shop and school, tells about a shark hunt he went on. John is not the type of diver who normally feels he has to prove himself by choosing risky situations. He doesn't mind admitting that he prefers good, easy conditions for his dives rather than difficult challenges. And he had absolutely no desire to meet a shark much less hunt one. But a group of his friends had become enthusiastic about shark hunting and insisted that he join them on a forthcoming trip. All the previous week, John kept trying to find a legitimate-sounding excuse for not going shark hunting, but he could come up with nothing.

That weekend the shark hunters left on a chartered boat out of Indian River Inlet in Delaware, in search of sand-tiger sharks. As they headed for the hunting area, John had a last hope. "Maybe I'll develop a superb case of seasickness," he thought. That was an excuse everyone would respect. Who could think him chicken for not getting in the water if he was busy vomiting over the side of the boat? No such luck, though; the water was calm and he felt fine.

At last they entered the water, armed with "bang sticks," poles bearing explosive charges in their heads. Aiming for the spine, the hunter would stick the pole against the shark, detonating the charge. John's apprehension vanished when he realized that the sharks were more scared than he was. Though his party killed a number of sharks, John failed to spear any. And as the boat returned to port, he swore to himself he'd never get into anything like that again. It wasn't the danger; it was the waste of killing sharks no one intended to eat.

I have a few shark stories I enjoy telling. One more properly belongs to Don Arrington, though I was there with him at the time. He, Benny Pannis, an ex-UDT diver, and I were wreck diving off the *Catherine E,* a 65-foot dive boat. We were in an area off the Delaware coast known as the Shoals. About ten other divers had come along on the boat, but Don, Benny and I had made a deal with the captain: We'd "set the hook"—place the anchor in the superstructure of the wreck —if he would give us the first 15 minutes in the water alone.

The nameless, World War II vintage wreck rested bottom down in only 35 feet of water. After setting the hook, the three of us swam along the low hull of the ship, which was mostly buried in the sand. With visibility only a few feet, we stayed close. We then drifted up to come over the deck, and as we did, we spotted blackfish. Most blackfish a diver finds are in the 2- to 10-pound range, but these looked to be at least

12 pounds. Benny motioned to me: "Too bad we don't have a speargun, should I go up and get one?" We were pondering this when the blackfish suddenly took flight. We assumed our bubbles must have scared them and moved along the deck hoping to find where they went.

We were swimming close together, with Don slightly ahead, when out of the corner of my eye I saw Benny stop and grab hold of a capstan on the deck. I asked by hand signal what was the matter. He hesitated, then pointed his finger at Don, who was turned toward us with his palms up, asking what was going on. I immediately saw what Benny had seen: Behind Don's head, a very big shark slowly slid out of the gloom. I didn't want to tell Don to look; I was afraid he might make some move that would disturb the shark. But Don saw we were looking behind him and turned around, rising slightly as he did, just enough to bump into the nose of the shark.

As Don tells it, "Something gave me a whack in the crown of the head—not serious. It felt like an elbow shot you get on a subway. I turned a little more and saw this tremendous yellow eye. Damn! I took one backstroke and saw the shark going by me . . . and going by me—just sliding by and sliding by. I thought it would never end. It was like watching a train from a station platform. The head had long ago disappeared into the murk by the time I saw the huge upright tail."

This called for a consultation. The three of us dropped to the sandy bottom next to the hull. We looked at each other only a brief second before three of our thumbs shot up, signalling, "Let's go up!" We backtracked along the side of the wreck, keeping close to the bottom. Occasionally one of us would pop his head above the low hull wall, swivel it around looking for the shark, and quickly pull it back. I began chuckling into my regulator, then laughing. I could hear Benny and Don laughing too. The sight of that monster plowing into one of us had stirred some deep primordial fear that each of us had succeeded in controlling. Now we were feeling the release, and it came out as laughter. I laughed so hard that my regulator kept falling out of my mouth, and I had to hold it in with my hand.

When we got to the anchor line, Don signalled to me, go ahead up. I signalled, you go first. Benny seemed happy to let us two decide who'd be first on the line. The bottom seemed safe; we were protected at least in one direction from a shark attack. The line would expose us, and we knew that breaking the water would be the most dangerous time, since splashing sounds draw sharks.

Finally we decided to go up the line together. We'd been down just about 15 minutes when we reached the surface, and the other ten divers were in the water swimming from the dive platform to the line. The captain saw us and called out, "What're you boys doing up so soon?"

"We didn't like the company," Don replied. "There's a big shark down there, a good ten and a half feet long."

On hearing that the other ten divers simultaneously made a U-turn to head back to the dive platform, full speed. It looked like a kickoff return formation—everyone heading in one direction then instantly cutting in another without having to look at their teammates.

That set us off again. The three of us flopped on the dive platform, laughing at the other divers as they scrambled over each other to get out of the water, not that I didn't know exactly how they felt.

On the way into port, we were drinking beer on the deck when one of the women divers said, "Come on, Jimmy, admit it. What you saw was a two-and-a-half-foot sand shark and you guys just panicked."

"Sure," I replied, "right now it's *our* shark story, so it's a two-and-a-half-foot sand shark. But wait till we get back. Then it'll become *your* shark story. You'll be the one who was down there. And that shark will have grown right back to ten and a half feet."

I've learned to distinguish among a few of the species of shark, and react to each accordingly. The sand shark can grow to lengths of eight feet and more, but those that East Coast divers encounter are usually much smaller. Though it has teeth capable of doing great damage, temperamentally the sand shark doesn't seem inclined to challenge humans. I don't challenge them, either, but I don't leave the water when I see one. The leopard shark, named for the black spots on its sides, is a small and relatively harmless shark found on the West Coast. One shark I would leave the water for is the blue shark, the most abundant one off the East Coast. Like most pelagic sharks, those that continuously cruise the open ocean rather than stay close to one home area, the blue can be very dangerous to men. Also common off the East Coast is the mako, a pelagic shark highly prized as a game fish since it makes spectacular leaps of 15 to 20 feet and swift runs of up to 40 miles an hour.

One shark I've never met and never hope to meet is the star of *Jaws,* the great white shark. If I ever do meet one and he attacks, I've already worked out my defense: I'll be reincarnated as a dolphin.

Terry Conmy and I were diving the clear Caribbean waters off Spanish Honduras during a trip aboard the 150-foot NASDS dive boat, the *Aquarius II.* Swimming through beautiful underwater canyons and coral formations, we came to a grotto, in 65 feet of water. We entered, and coral walls rose around us leading to a high ceiling. If fish were religious, this would be where they'd come on a Sunday. About eight feet up the wall projected a fine formation of elkhorn coral.

Terry had my Nikonos underwater camera and motioned for me to sit on the coral while she took my picture. I floated up and positioned myself while Terry readied the camera. She was slightly positive in her buoyancy and started to drift toward an overhang above her head. I motioned for her to watch her head so she let a little air out of her CBJ, a little too much for now she had to kick to keep up. Suddenly I saw a blast of sand two feet beneath where Terry's fins were kicking. An eight foot nurse shark had just been stirred from a nap, apparently by Terry's kicking. And Terry was drifting down toward its head.

A nurse shark is normally a docile creature—for a shark. However, the most docile of all God's creatures might become annoyed if it were napping in the sand and some alien kicked sand in its face, then attempted to step on its head.

I motioned for Terry to stop, just as she was taking the picture. Then I signalled, "Come here." "Why?" she asked.

I didn't want to tell her to look below, into the jaws of a shark. I knew she'd never seen a shark before, and I was afraid she might kick her fin right into its mouth in her hurry to get away.

"Come here!" I motioned again.

"Why?" she signalled with outstretched hands, as she fluttered just above the shark. Terry had been a student of mine, but now she was a fellow diver and good friend, and she didn't like being ordered around.

I swam down, grabbed her and, holding her against my chest, swam backward out of the grotto. Terry struggled and made unfriendly faces at me.

We were both running low on air and had to ascend. As soon as we were out of the water, I started to explain. "Look, Terry. . . ."

"Never mind, Jimmy," she snapped.

I decided to wait until she cooled down, then I'd tell her what I had saved her from. I was in the bar a little later when Terry entered. "Terry, listen. . . ."

"Look, Jimmy, I don't know who you think you are, but

if you've got something to tell me underwater, then tell me. Don't go grabbing me and dragging me around when you feel like it."

I'd been looking forward to the pleasure of delivering my punch line: "Okay, Terry, next time you're about to step on a shark's head, I'll just let you do it."

"What!? You mean there was a shark there when you dragged me out?"

"That's right."

"Why the hell didn't you tell me?"

"Well, I just didn't know how you'd react."

"Now am I going to find out how I'm going to react to a shark until I see one? You should have *told* me!"

That's what I like about the women who take up scuba diving. They're not timid damsels who need to be rescued from dragons or sharks. They're capable of doing for themselves. Still. . . .

The shark was here a long time before we were and will probably be here a long time after we're gone. Meanwhile, we hate them, not totally without reason. And often we kill them, usually without reason since they aren't generally looked upon as a fish to eat.

Recently, however, the Oyster Bar at Grand Central Station in New York began serving mako. It makes a fine dish, tastier than swordfish. And in England, the traditional British fish in fish 'n' chips is usually shark.

The second most voracious killer of the seas may soon be providing more food for the most voracious killer.

CHAPTER 15

SEA CREATURES, GREAT AND SMALL

The most fascinating thing about the sea is that it is alive, teeming with a fantastic variety of creatures. Maybe someday, in our insane pursuit of "progress" at any cost, humans will kill the seas. The great whales will be exterminated. The microscopic organisms that begin the sea's chain of life will be poisoned by industrial wastes and smothered by oil spills. But today at least, a diver can experience rich multitudes of animal and vegetable life that is adapted to a world so different from ours.

Where I grew up we didn't have many creatures above the size of cockroaches, except for mice, rats, dogs and cats. Almost everything that flew was a pigeon. But like most children, wherever they grow up, I learned enough about the animals that lived on land for them to seem familiar, or at least understandable. They breathed the same air and coped with the same law of gravity that I did. Sea life, except for the fish that appeared on my plate, remained something exotic and mysterious. I could see lions and elephants in the zoo, but nowhere could I see a shark or a whale.

Yet the sea, which covers 70 percent of the planet, has a wider and more interesting range of life than does the land. The largest living being that ever existed was not a dinosaur but the blue whale, threatened with extinction but still roaming the oceans. The most ferocious animal alive is not the lion but the shark. More strange and colorful fauna can be seen during one dive on a coral reef than during a week-long trek through a forest. Alice didn't have to fall down a rabbit hole to meet a spectrum of gaudy and weird creatures; she could have donned scuba gear and found her wonderland beneath the sea.

Of course, any sea animal appears less curious to a diver who has seen it many times. But even after a diver grows familiar with marine life in one area, he still has whole new worlds of life to learn about. And he doesn't have to travel to another continent for the experience. Each of the great bodies of water bordering this country—the Pacific, the Great Lakes, the Atlantic, the Caribbean and the Gulf of Mexico—has its own marine population mixture, with its own special attractions.

Take, for instance, one dive that I made in California when I was in commercial diving school. It was my first West Coast dive since the weekend before Vietnam, and my first dive in Northern California. I remember the dive with great clarity; every movement, every detail is still vivid in my mind's eye. I recall it so well because I met creatures which, though commonplace to California divers, were new and wondrous to me.

Larry Pike, a fellow student at the Coastal School who lived in San Jose, had invited me down to his family's home for a weekend of scuba diving. After saying hello to his family, we headed for Monterey Bay. When we arrived the winds and clouds which had been sweeping the area and causing rough water gave way to sunshine and calm seas.

Larry wanted to spearfish but I preferred just to sightsee. While he searched for our dinner, I floated by some rocks, looking through the crystal clear water and the lush green forest of kelp, when a bird swam by me. A *bird!* Thirty feet underwater! It paddled by, chugging through the water with its webbed feet, its long neck stretched out ahead. It grabbed a fish in its bill and swam back up. In another minute it dived down again.

The bird was a cormorant, a type of duck that can dive 35 or 40 feet for a fish. To Larry it was nothing new, but I was mesmerized by it. While Larry continued spearfishing, I just leaned against a rock and watched the birds diving for what must have been 15 minutes. I had known about diving birds, but I had just never thought about meeting a bird underwater.

We changed tanks and made our second dive, weaving our way through the kelp forest. About 300 yards offshore, we came to a large boulder that had been split in half. The crevasse through the rock must have been 15 feet long, and I began swimming through it. When I got halfway in, I met a large fish coming through from the other side. It measured about four feet, had black and white cross-hatchings on its back, black spots on its side and a large mouth—a leopard shark! I startled the shark as much as it startled me, and it was quicker. It turned around and ducked under a ledge. I had never met a leopard shark before, but I had recognized it by its distinctive markings, and I knew they rarely bothered divers. And the fact that it fled from me so quickly eased my brief nervousness.

Larry came up from behind me, and I pointed to the ledge, asking by hand signal if he had seen the shark. Sometimes hand signals aren't the best means of communication. Larry thought I was pointing out a fish for him to spear. He swam over to the ledge and poked his hand under it to chase the fish out. When the shark shot out and whizzed by, a few inches from his face, Larry's head jerked back and his eyes bulged. Then he looked at me and his expression said more than a hand signal ever could: "Ohhhh, so *that*'s what you were trying to tell me." Then we both began laughing so hard we had to come up for a breather. Funny, how sharks can make a diver laugh so much.

Later, we were swimming among rocks that projected out of the water, searching for abalone. In Northern California, it's illegal to take abalone while wearing scuba gear, but we were just reconnoitering, planning to come back and free dive from the rocks if we found an area with many good sized abs.

I noticed a sudden movement above me. I glanced up and saw a large dark shape plunging toward me. For a moment I was stunned with fright. Then I recognized it: a sea otter.

The only sea otters or seals I'd ever seen were in a zoo. Yet here one was, a fellow mammal joining me on a dive. He swam up to me and, seeming quite friendly, peered into my mask. Larry, who was used to sea otters and liked them, came over and petted him. The sea otter obviously enjoyed it but seemed to want something more from Larry. He kept waving his flippers as if clapping his hands, and giving Larry beseaching looks, like a dog begging for a scrap of food. Finally Larry caught on. The sea otter wanted to be fed. Larry picked up an abalone and handed it to the sea otter, who tucked it under one flipper and resumed clapping. Larry handed him another abalone, which the sea otter put under his other flipper. Still, he was clapping. Larry offered him a third ab, and then it occurred to the sea otter that he had no place to put a third one. Without a nod of thanks, he took off for the surface.

A few minutes later, the sea otter returned, waving his flippers again. Larry looked at me and shrugged. This is getting ridiculous, his expression seemed to say; we're trying to find abs for ourselves, not a sea otter. But we didn't want to appear unfriendly to our amphibious cousin. Larry started playing with him, poking and tickling him. I joined in the fun, rubbing the sea otter's stomach. He rolled over on his back, like a puppy, wiggling with pleasure. But no one likes to be tickled too roughly, and when Larry went a little too far, the sea otter reached his head around and nipped Larry on the hand. He didn't bite enough to hurt, just a little nip as if to say: "Hey man, that's enough tickling for now."

We stopped playing with our companion and resumed our search for abs. The sea otter followed us for another five minutes, and we wondered if we had acquired a pet. When we didn't feed him another ab, though, he finally abandoned us.

While I was enjoying all the creatures I met for the first time on this dive, Larry was enjoying my reactions to them. I knew how he felt. One of the great pleasures in diving is to guide others through a diving experience you've already had, especially introducing divers to marine life they haven't met before.

I once did some diving at John Pennekamp Coral Reef State Park off Key Largo, Florida. It was a miserable day and the water was rough when I arrived at the dive center to board the boat. Only two other divers were aboard, and the captain was surprised that even three of us had shown up. The other two, an Army captain and his wife from Minnesota, were on the last two days of their vacation. This was their first chance to dive the Keys, and they hadn't wanted to pass it up.

We chatted as the boat headed out. They told me they'd been diving for two years, but had never dived in salt water before, only in lakes. I discussed with them the amount of extra weighting they'd need in the salt water. And since I had dived the area before, I volunteered to guide them. I knew they would be excited by the marine life they'd be meeting for the first time, and I began looking forward to the dive even more.

After entering the water, we were exploring a sandy bottomed gap between two reefs, when I spotted a large sting ray lying in the sand ahead of us. I pointed toward it, but neither the captain nor his wife could see it lying in the sand. A sting ray doesn't look like any fish you'd find in a lake, and

I'm sure I couldn't have spotted this one too easily if I hadn't seen them before.

I motioned my companions on, and when we got within 12 feet of the ray, it lifted the sand off its wings and very gently took off, flying gracefully and easily. Then it landed about 30 feet ahead. The woman looked startled, and I guessed she had heard stories about the "deadly" sting ray and its poisonous, barbed tail.

Actually, the ray is a very harmless creature. Its stinger, which is minute and located near the base of its tail, serves purely as a defensive weapon. Only if a diver steps on a ray does the ray pose any danger to him. Then, in a reflex action, the ray will fling its tail upward, driving its bard into a diver's leg. The wound can get infected and cause trouble, but it is not, by normal standards, deadly. Divers entering from a beach, in an area with sting rays, shuffle sideways into the water, to avoid stepping on one. The shuffle will shove the sting ray out of the diver's way rather than trigger its defense mechanism.

I motioned for the captain and his wife to continue toward the ray, and this time when it took flight, I could see the delight in their eyes at the graceful motion, now that they felt confident the ray wouldn't attack them. The ray disappeared into the murk that the weather had stirred up, and we turned to explore in another direction. As we did, I spotted five or six barracuda, about a foot and a half in size.

The captain and his wife hadn't seen them yet, and I could remember how chilling the sight of a barracuda had been when I'd never met one before. As their guide I wanted to teach them about barracuda, but I didn't want them to spot the barracuda on their own, for they might become panicky. I tapped the wife on her shoulder and pointed at the bar-racuda. Her eyes grew wide, and she started to move back toward some rocks behind us, to hide behind them. But I motioned to them both: "Wait, stay where you are and watch me." I swam toward the barracuda and they backed off. I moved toward them again, and again they moved back. Then I swam to the captain and his wife, gestured to say, "See, they're harmless." I took her by the hand and swam with her toward the barracuda. She looked a little nervous, but she had decided to trust me, as obviously had her husband, and he swam along with us. We kept approaching the barracuda and they kept moving back, just out of our range. I could see the captain and his wife losing their nervousness and beginning to enjoy the game, pleased with themselves that they'd learned about a notorious fish. They'd heard such terrible things about barracuda, and now they had discovered the truth for themselves.

When we came up from the dive we were all grinning broadly. They'd had as good and interesting a time on their first saltwater dive as I had had on my first Northern California dive. And in both cases, it was because we met new marine life, and we had good guides.

With the exception of the shark and possibly the killer whale, no creature of the sea will bother a diver unless the diver bothers it. But the diver has to learn what actions of his might threaten a marine animal and thereby cause a defensive reaction. Ignorance is what gets divers into trouble with inhabitants of the sea. I always teach my students about the marine life of an area we're diving in, and I tell them to familiarize themselves with the local marine life in any diving area new to them. Little danger is presented to a diver by any creatures of the sea, *if* the diver knows about them.

Take, for instance, the lowly sea urchin. This pincushion of an animal can be found in many coastal areas, the West Coast and the tropics especially, but it is rarely seen in the Northeast. Inevitably, therefore, East Coast divers are the ones who wind up with the needle-sharp spines stuck in their knees when diving out of their home area. A diver has to learn that, when he kneels down to focus an underwater camera while shooting a wreck in Bermuda, he has to check beneath his knees for sea urchins burrowed in the sand. Many divers wrongly assume that a wet suit offers sufficient protection from these spines.

Another "dangerous" sea creature my students have to be warned about before traveling to Bermuda or the Caribbean on a diving trip, is fire coral. Coral is so beautiful that divers become careless about handling it. And even divers' gloves don't completely solve the problem. On one Bermuda trip that Don Arrington and I conducted, Kevin Burke, water sports director of Sonesta Beach Hotel, took our group on a dive to explore some coral reefs. Mickey Whalen, one of our divers, found some lovely, glowing pieces of coral that she put in her sea bag. Later, on the boat, she decided to look over her coral and shell collection. With her gloves off, she picked up the coral, let out a yelp and threw it overboard. By causing an allergic reaction, fire coral can inflict burns that last for days and even months.

One marine animal that my divers are familiar with is the jellyfish, frequently found off the shores of New Jersey and Long Island. These transparent sea monsters with stinging filaments come in many sizes. The nastiest of all is the Portuguese man-of-war, which is actually a colony of jellyfish. Wet-suited divers sometimes become overconfident and ignore jellyfish, knowing that they can't sting through a wet suit. If, however, a diver leaves the water with jellyfish filaments clinging to his wet suit, he might be stung as he removes the suit. That's one good reason for rinsing down a wet suit after a dive.

The moray eel can be dangerous but isn't nearly as dangerous as it looks. With fierce eyes and bared fangs, the moray seems quite fearsome; it has even been used for close-up shots in monster movies. But these eels are really just homebodies. Diving off Honduras and the Keys, I've run into quite a few,

A diver comes through a coral split off Eleuthra in the Bahamas. *(Photo by Jim Gott)*

projecting from their holes in the rock or coral. They stick out eight to ten inches, weaving menacingly in the current, but all they're doing is guarding their territory. If you stick your hand in a moray eel's hole, it will bite you. Otherwise the diver is safe. And a diver with half a brain would know better than to tempt the slender beast by attacking its hole.

Very few creatures of the sea present danger of any kind to the diver. In my marine environment lectures, warnings about possible dangers can be covered quickly, mostly with a few common sense rules. For the rest of the lectures, I prepare the group to recognize and enjoy the life they'll find in our diving area. When we enter the water I point out whatever interesting fish wander by. Once some fish even attended my lecture session.

It was a windy, rainy day in Newport, and before the class, the students piled into my van for some coffee. A couple of them expected the class to be called off, but I said, "You haven't learned about rough water conditions yet, and this is as good as any time to learn."

We donned our wet suits and went to the water's edge to cool down—splash water on our faces and down our suits to keep from overheating. I was kneeling in the shallow water when I saw some strange creatures in a tidal pool. They were squid, eight to ten inches long. Though divers often encounter squid, these were the first I'd seen in the waters off Newport. The storm apparently blew them in.

I give my lecture on marine life just before we enter the water. This time I announced we had live visitors, holding up a squid for them to see.

"Scungilli!" squealed one of my students, who happened to be Italian. I looked at the squid again. I'd never eaten one, but maybe it would be a tasty dish. However, I threw it back.

Intriguing as this ten-inch fish is, it has a more interesting relative that grows to 50 feet, one case in which the imaginative stories and movies about monsters of the deep aren't all

The beautiful scorpion fish can severely injure a diver with its venomous spines—if the diver bothers it. *(Photo by Jim Gott)*

fiction. Huge squid live at great depths, far beyond those that scuba divers or fishing lines reach. We know this because tentacles of giant squid have been found in the stomachs of sperm whales, which can dive to 3300 feet for their meals.

The octopus, which has a rounder head and two fewer tentacles than the squid, is a sea creature that has unfairly been given a bad name by the sea horror stories. Actually it's a very unthreatening fellow. Once on a night dive in Honduras, four of us came upon an octopus with about a three-foot tentacle spread, clinging warily to a rock. We tried to play with him, shaking hands and tickling him. The octopus didn't seem to enjoy the sport and decided that if he camouflaged himself, we'd go away.

First he turned himself a grayish color to blend into the sand. When we didn't let go, he decided he must have chosen the wrong color and changed himself to blue. That still didn't work. Finally he did hit on the right color. When the octopus turned a bright red and started swelling up, we decided that we were upsetting him too much and let go. The octopus shot away, ducking beneath some nearby rocks and leaving behind a jet of ink.

Contrary to the old stories, the ink is not a smoke-screen to blind pursuers; it doesn't spread over an area much larger than the octopus itself. It serves rather as a decoy, making the pursuer think that the ink itself is the octopus.

That's what I mean about marine life being so fascinating. What land creature knows such a clever trick?

CHAPTER 16

SAVING WHAT YOU SEE

Some years ago, diving in Shinnecock Inlet on Long Island, I was drifting slowly along the sandy bottom, observing the small marine inhabitants going through their routine struggles for existence. It's a habit of mine to move very slowly underwater at times, so I can look closely at the small scenes. Too many divers notice only the big picture and miss out on much of the fascinating world around them.

A baby lobster inching out of its hole caught my attention. I could see it reaching its large claw toward a detached crab leg. The lobster was much too small to eat so I wasn't tempted to put it in my bag. I released a little air from my CBJ and settled on the bottom to watch the little creature's effort to feed itself. It grabbed the leg and pulled it back toward its hole. But the lobster pulled the crab leg sideways and couldn't fit it into the hole.

I was intrigued. Could the lobster figure out that it should pull that tasty morsel lengthways? I decided to help out a little. I pulled the crab leg away from the lobster, to allow it to start on the problem fresh. The lobster scurried into its hole, then peeked out. When it didn't see me moving, it went back to its work. Again, it tried to pull the crab leg sideways, again failed, and again I pulled the leg away and waited for it to start again. I don't know how long this went on, but it must have been some time. I had plenty of air left when I spotted the lobster, and I went on reserve while still watching. One thing bothered me about the incident: I wished I had a picture of that lobster struggling with its evening meal.

I'd been an amateur photographer for years. As far back as the Boy Scouts, I had learned to develop my own film, even color. But at this time, only recently out of the Marines, I hadn't yet begun taking photographs underwater. I knew that the kind of camera equipment that I would want was expensive, and I had been spending my money on scuba gear. Now, though, I had to get started on underwater photography.

Not long after that, I ran into Don Arrington, who at that time hadn't yet become underwater photography instructor at the school. I knew he was a first-rate underwater photographer and began discussing it with him. Don showed me some of his work. What impressed me most was his macrophotography, close-up views of marine life. That fit in so well with my attitude toward looking at things underwater. I always tell my students to stick their face plates right up to an object—a coral reef, a small section of the bottom—and they'll be fascinated by what they see; the beauty and drama of life exist even in a handful of water. Photography is a way of seeing things and Don's view of the underwater world coincided so well with mine that I asked him to teach me how to adapt my land photography knowledge to the underwater. And he did.

Now, after several years of learning from an excellent instructor, I can handle the most sophisticated equipment and take what I consider good photos fairly consistently. It has become one of my prime underwater interests, and I try to pass my knowledge and enthusiasm for it on to fellow divers and students.

Major advances have been made in underwater photography in the past few years, especially in cinematography. Anyone who has seen Jacques Cousteau's television specials or the films *Blue Water, White Death; Jaws* or *Shark Treasure* knows just how sophisticated underwater moviemaking has recently become. But neither still nor motion picture photography underwater is as new a field as one might suppose. A Frenchman named Louis Boutan took undersea photographs as early as 1893, and he published a book, *Undersea Photography,* in 1900. The first underwater movies were made back in 1914 by J.E. Williamson, an American. But the development of modern scuba, especially the scuba boom of the last decade, has brought underwater photography out of the realm of an oddity and established it as a major branch of the art. And it has made the underwater world available to millions of amateur photographers.

Even an inexperienced photographer can take respectable underwater pictures by using an automatic exposure camera like the Instamatic encased in an inexpensive waterproof plexiglas housing. By eliminating almost all possibilities of human error, the Instamatic enables the photographer to take consistently passable photographs, if the diver chooses his subjects and conditions correctly. On one diving trip to Bermuda, a young nurse with an Instamatic wound up with far better photographs than did a veteran diver with thousands of dollars worth of equipment.

While the Instamatic allows for little human error, it drastically limits a photo-diver's flexibility. Instamatic photographers, whether on dry land or underwater, can reach a certain level of expertise. But if a diver has a serious interest in photography, he'll soon tire of the plateau he reaches where all his photos begin to look alike. He will go on to more sophisticated equipment. In the beginning, the trial and error process of learning about progressively more sophisticated equipment can be very frustrating, and the photographer may make more errors and ruin many shots. But the better the equipment, the greater flexibility the photographer has and the more control over his photography. And that's the aim of the real shutterbugs, wet or dry.

The camera that most underwater photographers choose, whether serious amateurs or professionals, is the Nikonos, which was designed for the scuba diver. This 35mm camera requires no waterproof housing, which means that it's much smaller than comparable 35mm cameras that need housing for underwater use.

One major difference between above- and below-water photography is in the amount of light available. Since water reflects light, the intensity of light decreases with depth. And the choppier the water, the more light is deflected. Because of the difficulty in estimating the amount of light underwater, photodivers who don't have automatic exposure cameras have to rely on light meters. Some divers use regular light meters sealed in watertight jars for underwater use. However, submersible light meters are available at reasonable prices, and most serious underwater photographers use them.

Underwater, everything appears 25 percent larger and 25

Negatively buoyant, photographer Frank Fennell steadies himself for his shot. *(Photo by Jim Gott)*

percent closer, due to the refraction of light passing first through the water and then through the air in the face mask and the eye itself. Divers get into habit of automatically correcting this distortion. A fish that appears to be 15 feet away the diver knows is actually 20 feet away. Divers new to underwater photography often make the mistake of setting the camera distance for the real distance as he knows it, rather than the apparent distance. Due to the air behind the lense, the camera itself sees in the same way the human eye does. So the diver must remember to set the camera at the apparent distance rather than the real one.

Distance is difficult to work with in another way. What may look like a clear view of some subject 30 feet away can turn out to be very blurry in a photo. The camera eye picks up more of the minute particles suspended in water than does the human eye. The best practice is to shoot only subjects that are within one-fourth of the maximum visibility.

Another major difference between above- and underwater photography is the fact that water filters out colors. At 15 feet, red begins to dull and at 25 feet it is almost completely absorbed. Orange vanishes at 35 feet, then yellow and green. Blue is the only color remaining below 100 feet; everything else is black or white or gray.

Shooting color film in natural light, the diver can partially restore the colors by using a red filter. This filter holds back the blues and greens while letting through more of the warm colors, the red, yellow, orange and brown tones. A red filter can also improve black and white film by enhancing contrasts.

Though divers learning underwater photography should start out using natural light, the most dramatic possibilities for photography come with artificial underwater lighting. Photography is a way of seeing things, but beneath the sea a flashbulb unit or a strobe (electronic flash) does more than that. It enables a diver to see colors underwater that are invisible to the naked eye.

A diver takes a strobe along with him to photograph a grayish-blue reef 100 feet down. He lines up an interesting looking shot, and when he fires, colors explode around him for one blinding instant. Then everything resumes its blue or gray tones. He develops his picture and sees an amazing scene, one he has seen before only for one giddy instant: a reef and the fish around it alive with all the colors of the rainbow. It's hard for the diver to believe that it's the same grayish-blue reef he had been exploring for 15 minutes.

Do color photographs reveal underwater life as it really is or change it to an unreal appearance? Is the color really there without an artificial underwater light to reveal it? The question is as unanswerable as: When a tree falls in a forest and no one hears it, does it make a sound? I do know, however, that once you've begun shooting with strobe lights underwater, you're always anxious to see any potentially colorful deep-water scene in its "true" colors.

Composition can give underwater photographers trouble until they learn a few rules. Divers are used to looking at things from above, and the natural tendency therefore is to shoot down at a subject. But this doesn't result in good pictures; shot against the bottom, the subject tends to blend into the background, especially in black and white photos. Most photos should be shot level, at a slight upward angle, or toward the surface. A surface shot can result in the dramatic effect of the subject being silhouetted against the surface light. Shooting level or slightly upward provides a greater separation of subject from background, more contrast, which is what most photographers want.

Sometimes too little attention is paid to the importance of diving skill in underwater photography. No one can be an accomplished underwater photographer without being a good diver. Some degree of diving experience and ability is

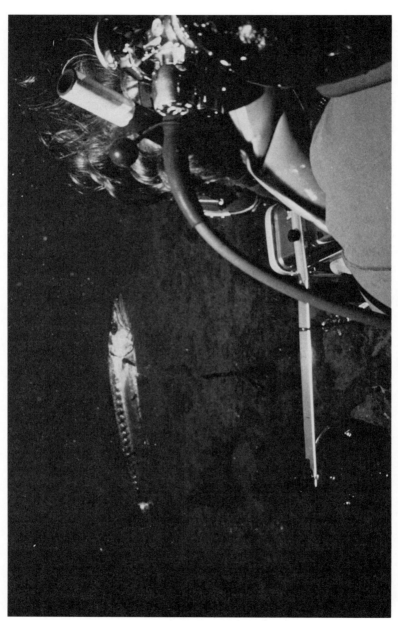

Trying to get a barracuda to stay still for a photograph is no easy matter. *(Photo by Joseph Payne)*

required just to enable a diver to find his underwater subjects, be they coral formations or fish. It takes excellent control for a diver to stalk a fish for a shot or to lower himself quietly to the bottom near a photogenic fish without scaring it off. He must be able to move gracefully and adjust his buoyancy to the most minute degree. Most important, in order to see and photograph it clearly, the diver–photographer has to feel comfortable in the underwater world.

And being at home underwater is what diving itself is all about.

CHAPTER 17

DARKER, COLDER, FASTER, DEEPER

All divers have at least one thing in common: They're more adventurous than the average person. Otherwise they would never have had the desire to enter the underwater world. And the impulse that led them into scuba diving often leads them further—into darker waters, colder waters, faster waters, deeper waters. As an instructor, I want scuba divers to be prepared for these more difficult and challenging areas.

My favorite advanced class is night diving. To me, the nighttime offers some great diving. When I dive at night a special sense of serenity comes over me. Though I'm always with a diving buddy, I feel very alone but at peace with the world around me. With my light out, I run my hand through the surface waters and see the microscopic marine life—plankton and diatoms—sparkle with luminescence.

I remember a night dive in Bermuda. I finned through clear shallow water on a moonlit night and below me a reef came alive with glowing eyes. They were skipper lobsters, a small shellfish that can rarely be seen by day because their color perfectly matches the reef. At night their eyes reflect the moonlight, or the diver's handlight, making the reef look like a galaxy.

You see different life at night than during the day. Lobsters, crabs and eels, which generally hide themselves by day, scurry around scavenging for food. Fish that hunt actively by day can be seen sleeping at night—some sleep upside down. Blackfish can be found in rock crevices, swaying back and forth in the current.

I often go night diving with a date. We drive down to the ocean in my van and enter the water from the beach. We come out with a load of lobsters, and head back to my apartment for an early breakfast of lobster and scrambled eggs.

Though I am relaxed diving at night, I know that the dark can bring out the worst fears in novice divers. They don't know what's around them in that blackness—perhaps the things that go bump in the night. In the course I teach, night diving is class five, the last mandatory class in the advanced open-water certification program. Every diver should make his first night dive only under very controlled circumstances. Even when he is experienced and well able to handle himself during the day, if he has never made a night dive he may find it a very frightening experience.

I take a maximum of four students on a dive boat out of City Island, New York. Each of us has his own light, and we head away from the boat with all our lights on. Then, before taking them down, I tell them that when I flash my light at each student, he has to turn his light off. We descend about 30 feet to the bottom, and I put them all in a circle, knees touching so I'll be able to feel any sudden movement, which sometimes means someone trying to bail out for the surface. One-by-one the lights are turned out, until we're kneeling in total darkness, the darkest dark that there is. Few people realize that they're almost never in total darkness; a dim reflection of light glimmers from somewhere even on the darkest night. But now the students are in darkness few have ever experienced.

We sit there for about two minutes, while I wait for the darkness to get to them. Their breathing rates go up, but being able to touch people on both sides helps them control the impulse to panic. Then I have them turn on their lights and we make a compass run. By now, their sense of direction is totally disoriented by the darkness, and they're convinced, as I have told them, that they have to rely on the compass, even if the direction "feels wrong."

Various students on a night dive have their own special fears, but many of them now focus their worries on the shark that lurks just out of range of the light beam. Once while I was leading a night-diving class, on the far range of my light beam I spotted a shark. It was just a sand shark, generally harmless, but I knew the chances of panic if my students saw it. I quickly shot the light to my left and shifted directions, neglecting to inform them about the shark. If they'd known they were in the water with any kind of shark, they'd have kept aiming their lights behind them to see if their legs were still there. Had it been a blue shark, a tiger or a mako, I would have taken them out of the water, but not for a sand shark.

When divers get over their fears, they are often excited by the colors they see on a night dive, especially when they dive tropical waters. With artificial illumination underwater, colors aren't filtered out as they are during the day. When a diver aims his light at a reef that looks blue-gray by daylight, it shows up, like in a flashlit photo, in all its colorful glory.

As an added bonus on my night-diving classes, I help my students to a special treat. I know a student will hesitate before grabbing a lobster for the first time, for fear the big claw might grab him. I show them how to grab the lobster, and I always wind up gathering enough for my class—not more than I'm sure they'll eat, though. And if someone wants to cook up the batch when we get to shore, I might even buy the wine.

Our school also offers an ice-diving class in our advanced course, but I rarely teach that one. I know some divers who find diving under ice especially appealing. To me, it's something to be tried occasionally for change of pace or when a diver can't get away to a warmer climate.

Our shop runs ice dives at Lake Minnewaska, 100 miles north of New York City. The first time I went, we traveled by bus on a snowy Friday evening in January and stayed that night at a hotel on the edge of the lake. A few of the group partied late, but most of us knew to save the partying until after diving. Early the next morning we gathered on the frozen lake and used a chain saw to cut a square hole in the ice, large enough for two divers to surface at the same time. The eight-by-eight chunk that we cut was then shoved under the adjoining ice, so we could replace it after the dive; it would be marked with flags to warn off ice fishermen, ice boats or snowmobiles until it froze solid again.

Meanwhile a tent was pitched and a fire was built. The dive master and his buddy entered the water first to run the safety line to the bottom. If we had any inexperienced divers in the group we would have used lines attached to the divers' waists, with a tender on top "fishing" the diver. Since all the divers in our group were veterans, we just used one safety line, which all divers would stay near.

On most dives, a diver breathes through his regulator to test it out just before getting into the water—but not on an ice dive. In the 15-degree weather, the moisture from our breath might have frozen the regulator valves. While a safety diver stood by, two of us at a time sat on the edge of the ice, then slipped into the water. The water didn't feel as cold as I had expected. In fact the temperature, in the low forties, wasn't much lower than the bottom of a freshwater lake or quarry in the summer. But, summer or winter, that temperature is cold enough to quickly drain the warmth from the diver's body when he's dressed in an ordinary one-quarter-inch wet suit. Ice dives tend to be of short duration.

The most striking thing about diving under the ice is the

crystal clarity of the water. The sheet of ice protects the fresh water from being stirred up by wind, as it is during the summer, and the algae which clouds lake waters in warm weather doesn't flourish in the cold. On this dive, the water had a glow to it, from the diffused sunlight coming through the ice. From underwater the hole looked dazzlingly bright compared to the rest of the ice-covered surface. Above us our bubbles hit against the bottom of the ice and formed air pockets.

I was aware of the ice above me and of having no surface exit except for one eight-by-eight foot hole, but I didn't find that knowledge disturbing. Eventually, though, I began to feel the chill of the water, and then we ascended. The toughest part of the dive was smashing through the 15-degree air as we ran to the tent. We quickly warmed ourselves with brandy while stripping off the wet suits next to the fire.

I have to admit that, as far as I was concerned, the best time during the whole dive trip was that evening when the partying began for all of us.

One thing a diver rarely experiences underwater is speed. It's a very slow world down there for humans. Fish of all sizes race by the diver as if he's standing still. And he practically is, even compared to his normal walking speed. He moves only at one knot, slightly more than one mile per hour, swimming at a normal pace, and rarely more than 2.2 knots even when he's swimming along as fast as he can.

The only occasion when a diver goes much faster is when he is caught in a current. Usually, that's not an experience a diver welcomes. A two- or three-knot current underwater will carry a diver with it, whether he wants to go in that direction or not. A diver should never fight a current. The best he could do by swimming against it would be to stay in the same place, at the expense of extreme exertion and greatly increased air consumption. The current has plenty of time to get where it's going, and the diver doesn't. Unless the current is a narrow stream and the diver can angle his way into calmer water nearby, he should lie back and let the current take him where it will. The result can be inconvenient—taking the diver far away from the dive boat, for instance—but a current, especially a rip current just off a beach, doesn't usually carry a diver too far before he can escape from it.

It's a different story if the diver knows about the current and chooses to ride it. That can make for a very thrilling dive.

One of the great places in the world for drift diving, riding a current, is the island of North Eleuthera in the Bahamas. A half-mile-long, 75-yard-wide channel cuts through an arm of the island, and millions of gallons of water pour through this channel each hour, alternating directions with the tide. The current runs around seven knots, far more than a diver ever encounters in the open ocean.

On one dive trip to the Bahamas, I rode that Eleuthera cut. Five of us from our dive group took Bob Ollier's 50-foot dive boat *Hobo* to the Current Cut late on an August afternoon. Before Bob dropped us at the mouth of the cut, he told us to spend only five minutes underwater, then surface. If we took longer, we'd go into a shallow area his boat couldn't reach. When he cut the engine, we had to get into the water, deflate and head down immediately, because he had to start up his engine quickly to keep from being pulled by the current into the side of the cut.

Bob dropped us to the right side of the cut, but I had planned with Frank Fennell, my diving buddy who had recently become a fellow instructor at the Skin Diving School of New York, to work our way over to the left. Other divers had told us that was the more interesting side. We found ourselves on a flat sandy bottom. Around us were immense starfish, which must have measured three feet across. The current grabbed us and swept us along. We could see the bottom rushing by below us. Around us were fish of all kinds: amberjacks, parrot fish, yellow tails, hog fish, hake. Some were drifting with us; others were hiding behind rocks to avoid being pulled by the current. Perhaps they were waiting for the tide to change. There was no way for us to battle the current directly, but we managed to angle our way to the left by strenuous effort, using a lot of air. When we just rode with the current, we hardly used any air at all.

We were swept along walls of a canyon that dropped from 30 to 60 feet down, and just when it seemed we'd be slammed against the side, the current pushed us away. It was like riding a toboggan to the crest of a sloping wall, then being shot down again. In the bottom of one canyon, hundreds of dead conch lay in a hole, apparently trapped there by the torrent.

Then I saw a seven foot barracuda ahead of us, facing into the current, gently moving its tail. It had such sheer power and grace that it hardly seemed to make any effort just hanging there. It was probably waiting for prey to be swept into its mouth. Neither of us wanted to be prey, and as the barracuda loomed ahead of us, I rolled my body to the left, Frank rolled his to the right, and we passed the barracuda between us. Then it was time to head up.

The five of us met on the surface and waved the orange gloves Bob had given us so he could be sure to spot us in the fading light of the afternoon. With our CBJs inflated as we drifted along together, waiting for the boat, Frank commented that it didn't seem as if we were moving at all as long as we were looking at each other. But when we glanced down, we could see the bottom hurrying beneath us.

After Bob picked us up, he took us back for a second run. Frank and I wanted to work our way back into the canyon in the center of the cut. I grabbed hold of an old pipe that ran along the edge of the canyon and tried to pull myself over the side and down. Holding to the pipe I could feel the full force of the current, jerking and pulling me in its direction. My mask was partly ripped off, and I had to hold on to the pipe with one hand, while trying to clear my mask with the other. The water rushing up the canyon walls was too strong for us. We couldn't pull ourselves against it. Finally, we let go and drifted with the torrent which rushed us along to our second rendezvous with the boat.

To travel as fast as a fish was an exhilarating experience.

Depth lures divers. Not diving deep for the sake of seeing a fascinating wreck or coral reef way down, but just diving deep to see how deep you can go. It's not sensible: Most everything worth seeing in an ocean can be found in the first hundred feet. It's not safe: The Navy puts its limit on safe scuba diving at 132 feet. Deeper than that and the diver runs into the risk of nitrogen narcosis which can endanger his life. Most scuba divers have heard the story about the narced diver who worried that a passing fish was without an air supply and offered it his regulator—then drowned.

In basic classes I tell my students that there are no compelling reasons to go deep enough or stay long enough underwater to require decompression on the way up; they can have enjoyable diving without ever doing so. But, I also teach the decompression tables and urge the use of decompression meters. Our advanced diving course offers deep and repetitive diving classes. We know that most experienced divers will be making decompression dives, seeking the challenge of depth. And some will go too deep for safety.

I was with Bill Whalen, known as "The Whale" despite his slim physique, diving off Spanish Honduras. We were cruising over a reef some 25 feet down, when we came to a sheer wall where the reef ended. Diving down a wall can be very exciting. It gives you a sense of flying to have a reference point alongside you. I signalled to Bill, "Let's head down." The water had the kind of sunny clarity typical of the Caribbean, a clarity that can deceive you about depth. Novice divers have often gotten into trouble, wandering into dangerous depths without knowing how deep they were. But Bill and I had our depth gauges, and we kept checking them.

As we descended the wall, I decided that I wanted to go deep, very deep. As an instructor, students had often asked me about very deep diving and I'd told them about its dangers, but I'd never experienced it, not beyond 200 feet. But I wanted to. And, however foolish or risky it might be, I felt this was the time to do it.

At 150 feet, Bill pointed to his camera, indicating he wanted to stop and take a picture. I motioned, "No, let's keep going." I pointed to the maximum depth reading on my depth gauge: 250 feet. Bill gave me the okay sign. We both had plenty of air. The only way we'd get into trouble would be by narcing. I had experienced nitrogen narcosis in test chambers back at Coastal School, and I knew its symptoms. I knew Bill. We'd dived many times together, and we had confidence in each other as diving buddies. We had that kind of rapport that two good divers can acquire after many hours together underwater, immediately understanding even without hand signals what the other is doing, how he's feeling, almost to the point of ESP. We'd keep checking ourselves and each other for trouble and head back up if either of us seemed to be narcing.

We passed 200, sliding down the wall into the depths, then 225 feet. I planned for us to stop at 250 only long enough to take some photographs, then head back up. But when the meter read 250, we could see a ledge about 35 feet below us. I still felt fine and Bill seemed totally in control of himself too, so I pointed to the ledge: "We'll take the pictures down there." We landed on the ledge, 285 feet down. I watched closely as he snapped the picture and advanced the camera, and I could tell that he was still clear headed. He handed the camera to me and I took his picture. Then we headed up.

I was pleased with myself that I had no symptoms of nitrogen narcosis. Being narced is often compared to being drunk, but in most ways this is not an accurate comparison. The effects, chemically and psychologically, of nitrogen and alcohol are very different. However, the diver can control his narcing in much the same way a drinker can control how drunk he feels. Many drunks have found that they could sober up very quickly when they had to, and a diver in danger of narcing can fight against it by an exercise of his will. If the diver is aware of what is happening, he can—to some degree at least—demand of his body and mind that they keep functioning properly and not let the nitrogen narcosis gain control.

Then at 180 feet I saw a red sponge. Red? I looked again. Yes, it was red. Impossible, of course, since water filters out the color red before 25 feet, much less 180 feet. Yet there it was, red. Well, maybe I am getting a little narced, I thought to myself.

When we neared the surface we headed for the boat. Neither of our decompression meters were in the red zone, but we knew that the meters weren't geared for 285 feet. Rather than take a chance on getting the bends, we'd spend some time underwater decompressing. We each had about ten minutes of air left when we reached the anchor line. We hung there until we ran out, then came up to the dive platform and yelled for fresh tanks. While the crew was fetching them, Bill turned to me and asked, "What color was that sponge?"

"Did it look red to you, too?" I said.

"Yep."

We grabbed our tanks, without bothering to put them into our harnesses, and headed back down the anchor line for more decompression time. Some divers stay active while decompressing, believing that they can work the nitrogen out of their systems faster that way. My method is to keep still and do the kind of deep breathing used in yoga exercises, which purges the residual air in the lungs. As I was hanging from the line straight as a tin soldier, with a tank held between my legs, breathing a strange pattern of bubbles, I attracted the attention of some divers below us. One pair of buddies came over to ask if I was okay. "Okay," I signalled them. Then another pair came swimming up, and one offered me her octopus regulator to breathe from. "No, I'm okay," I signalled.

I was pleased by the attention, because it meant that these divers, all from our school, stayed aware of other divers in the water. Even though I had my buddy with me, they noticed what seemed to be unusual actions so they came to check on my safety.

After we came up, Bill and I told the others about the red sponge. We knew both of us could not have been narcing at the same time in the same peculiar way. Another pair of divers went down to look, and they brought it up. Though the sponge appeared grayish in the light, both divers assured us that it had glowed red down below. The sponge obviously was luminescent, which explained how it could appear red 180 feet down.

After finding out about the sponge, I decided that I had really sensed no affects from the nitrogen. Bill thought he felt some but only briefly. We both concluded that diving with someone we trusted made us less anxious about the depth and probably less subject to the effects of the nitrogen.

But narcing does happen to the best of divers. The day after our dive, Bill was down with Leroy Bonaparte, a very capable diver, and two others. They were diving at 150 feet, then they all decided, by hand signal, to head for the surface. They began to ascend, except for Leroy—he stayed at the same level and swam around in circles. Bill, his partner, went up to him and again signalled: "Up!" Leroy signalled back: "Up!" Then he continued swimming around in circles. Bill motioned to the other two divers to join him. The three of

The water looks good as I prepare to dive Smith's Cay near St. Thomas, Virgin Islands. *(Photo by Bill Gleason)*

them grabbed Leroy and led him up. Later, on the boat, Leroy explained: "I knew what you were signalling, but the way my mind was operating, I really thought I was headed up. I couldn't understand why you were acting so concerned."

Sometimes a diver can find new experiences underwater just by using his imagination.

Before joining the New York City Police Department, Don Arrington was a jump master in the 82nd Airborne. After he left the service, he took up skydiving and became quite an enthusiast. Then he hurt his back in an auto accident and his doctor warned him not to skydive again. That was when he took up scuba.

I have done some skydiving myself, and once on a diving trip, Don and I began discussing the techniques used in skydiving. Then we decided to try them in scuba. Pretty soon we evolved a style of descent closely imitating a sky dive. We release all the air from our jackets, and begin descending feet first, faster and faster. We turn over and with arms outspread, control our motions, as in a skydive, with slight turns of the hands. We can slow the descent by arching our backs. When we see the bottom coming up, we pull the ripcord—push the inflate button on the vest—and glide gently to the bottom.

In the underwater world, there's always something new to try. And acrobatics are safer—and more fun—than a 285-foot dive.

CHAPTER 18

PIONEERING THE MOST IMPORTANT FRONTIER

I believe that scuba diving is more than just another recreational activity. In a way no other sport or recreation can, it expands a person's boundaries and satisfies important psychological needs.

Most people wish for more freedom in their lives. They feel trapped by their jobs and powerless in the face of the political, social and economic forces that control them. They look for escape, and some find it underwater.

Ask any scuba diver what he enjoys about it, and one of the first words he'll probably use is "freedom." Beneath the seas, the diver enters a totally new world. He flies, unburdened even by the law of gravity. His every movement has a feeling of freedom to it. There's no traffic to dodge, no noise to deafen him, no one to hassle him.

The undersea world is a place that each diver chooses for himself. No one is forced into scuba diving by peer pressure or school athletic programs. No coaches are there underwater to tell a diver what to do. Once he learns the sport, the diver is on his own in it, free to enjoy it in his own way, at his own pace.

Even after years of diving, each new dive is still an adventure. And adventure is something many people need and look for in their lives. Scuba provides escape from a frustrating world, but the escape isn't mindless or passive. The diver has new sights and experiences to stimulate and challenge him. He encounters a dramatically different world, with different sets of rules.

One of the differences is that the world under the seas demands cooperation rather than competition. Most sports are strictly competitive. We exercise our skills for the purpose of defeating someone else. But most of us get all the competition we need in the everyday world. And it becomes a pleasure to escape to a world where survival itself depends on close cooperation with a buddy. Instead of trying to beat him, you're sharing with him.

Many people feel frustrated by the technology of our age. Mechanical forces always seem to be getting beyond our control. The car we depend on to get to work breaks down; the television that entertains us stops working; trains and elevators we ride grind to a halt, trapping us between stations or floors. We come to resent the way we depend on all the technology our civilization provides. Many escape by taking up backpacking, canoeing, camping or mountain climbing.

But scuba is different. The diver escapes from technological civilization into a natural environment, with the aid of a mechanical device that is fully under his control. Unlike televisions or automobiles, the device is simple enough to master and understand without much mechanical aptitude.

All these pleasures of scuba diving are shared by a community of divers that is growing at a rate approaching a quarter of a million a year, and one of the pleasures of being a diver is in belonging to this new and growing community. It's a fraternity that is open to everyone who chooses it. Once you know someone is a diver, you know you have something important in common with him or her that transcends differences in sex, race, jobs, education, religion or politics.

It's unfortunate that this sense of community hasn't always operated on the national level. The four national scuba training organizations—YMCA, NAUI, NASDS and PADI

—have all too often bickered among themselves, competing for students and prestige within the diving world.

Then, in 1974, something happened to change the spirit of competition into one of cooperation. Los Angeles County passed a County Scuba Diving Ordinance, introducing government regulation into the sport of diving for the first time. Concern over diver safety combined with failure to carefully examine scuba diving's safety record led to the passing of this law. The county government assumed the responsibility for allowing or prohibiting individuals to scuba dive, according to whether the person met a set of qualifications. For instance, a diver had to have 12 dives a year or he was prohibited by law from diving the following year unless he underwent a recertification examination. Also, if a diver had a beer with his lunch at noon, then went diving at 5:30 that afternoon, he violated the law. And he could be fined $500 and be sent to prison for six months, even for a first violation.

In many fields government regulations are necessary. But there's a limit to these areas. And diving is not a proper field for government control. Diving with scuba is not like driving a car; a scuba diver can endanger his own life, but he's not going to run someone over with his scuba gear. A government has no more business regulating scuba than it would in demanding that everyone who goes swimming or skiing must first pass a legislated set of requirements.

The scuba world, which felt that with few exceptions it had been doing a good job of self-regulation, joined in opposing the new law. Differences among YMCA, NAUI, NASDS and PADI were forgotten, and the four organizations got together to form a National Scuba Training Council. The purpose of this council is to develop a common set of standards in scuba training and self-regulation and to present a united front to misguided politicians who want to impose government control.

Then in September, 1975, the new council won its battle.

The Los Angeles County Board of Supervisors voted to repeal almost all of the provisions of the scuba ordinance. In the end, the ordinance helped the scuba diving community. The national unity it gave us can be valuable in dealing with more than just government regulation. It can provide the community of scuba divers with a united voice to promote the sport and, most important, to lobby for the protection of the ocean environment.

When astronauts first walked on the moon, breathing air from a pack on their backs and bouncing in the nearweightlessness, a great frontier had been conquered. But the promises of that frontier do not match the untapped potential of the sea. Water covers 70 percent of the Earth's surface, and this is where we will find the resources we need for the future of our planet. Like the moon, the underwater world is a very different environment from the one we're used to. Men must bring their own atmosphere with them and learn to cope with a different strength of gravity. But we don't need a billion-dollar space program to venture into this world.

We're still in the Stone Age in our exploitation of the sea. We hunt the animal life, but in few cases do we breed it. We have only begun to take advantage of the food potential of the ocean's vegetation. And most of the mineral wealth of the oceans has yet to be tapped. Of the 15 billion barrels of oil produced each year, about 20 percent comes from offshore production, and in five years that percentage may double. Scattered over the ocean bottom are nodules of copper, nickel, manganese and cobalt, enough to supply Earth's needs for generations. Within a few years, a suction device will be ready for use which can retrieve these nodules from 15,000 feet down.

As we begin to develop this new frontier, however, we must learn to respect the ocean's life systems and to use its wealth in ways that benefit all people, including future generations. If we allow a few greedy economic powers to exploit the wealth of the oceans only for their own profit, the oceans may be destroyed. That danger already exists.

Men have used the ocean as a garbage dump for too long. The waste dumped by East Coast cities, plus discharges from oil tankers, have combined to form a sludge of oil and plastics covering one million square miles of the Atlantic. Radioactive wastes are buried at sea in concrete drums that may not remain leak-proof forever. Marine life of all kinds have been poisoned by our chemical wastes.

The Audubon Society has noted increasing numbers of what are called "aquatic anomalies": birds flying erratically as if dizzy, then plunging into the sea; poisoned sea lions crawling up California beaches and traveling a mile inland before dying. Jacques Piccard, the Swiss oceanographer, warns that if the current direction doesn't change, life in the seas will be extinguished within two or three decades. And if that happens, life on land will soon follow.

So far we have come up with few solutions to the pollution and misuse of the oceans. International agreements are essential, but the last attempt to obtain cooperation among nations, the International Conference on the Law of the Sea in Geneva, ended in failure.

Human society has to wake up to the fact that the oceans provide the key to our future, and we have to stop wasting and poisoning them. I believe that scuba divers, as pioneers in the underwater frontier, can play an important role in that awakening. Scuba diving fosters the kind of awareness of the ocean environment that is needed. A diver learns to identify with the undersea world and appreciate its inhabitants. He becomes a conservationist just to defend his recreational area against those who would blindly destroy it. He knows the problems of oil sludges and pollution at first hand.

Not all scuba divers are as sensitive to conservation problems as they should be; marine life has disappeared from some reefs because of reckless spearfishermen. But the overwhelming majority of divers treat the underwater world with respect. Many are in the forefront of conservation activities.

Jacques Cousteau has long been one of the most important spokesmen for marine conservation, and his attitudes have filtered down to almost all of us who've followed him into the underwater world. For instance, among the membership of The Oceanic Society, an organization dedicated to the protection of the oceans and oceanic life, you'll find many scuba divers. I know because I've recently been active in helping the society organize a Long Island Sound chapter.

I consider the underwater world my second home. I want others to share with me my enjoyment of scuba diving. And all of us in the community of divers can join in promoting and protecting what is not only a great recreational area, but the future of our planet.